# The Dynamics of Biblical Counseling

Dr. Nicolas Ellen

# The Dynamics of Biblical Counseling

Copyright © 2009 by Dr. Nicolas Ellen

All rights reserved in all countries. No part of this material may be reproduced, stored in a retrieval system, or transmitted in any form or by any means electronic, mechanical, photocopying, recording, or otherwise without prior written permission of the author, publisher and/or copyright owners, except as provided by USA copyright law.

Readers may order copies by visiting www.mycounselingcorner.com

Published and Printed By Expository Counseling Center
Houston, Texas

Unless otherwise noted, scripture references are taken from the New American Standard Bible. © The Lockman Foundation, 1960, 1962, 1963, 1968, 1971, 1972, 1973, 1975, 1977.

**Publisher's Cataloging in Publication**

**Ellen, Nicolas:** *The Dynamics of Biblical Counseling*
1. Counseling  2. Christian Counseling  3. Christianity  4. Discipleship

ISBN 978-0-9779691-0-4

# THE DYNAMICS OF BIBLICAL COUNSELING
# TABLE OF CONTENTS

**5** *Section One*: What Makes Biblical Counseling Biblical, Qualifications of a Biblical Counselor (Watch Counseling Video #1)

**9** *Section Two*: Every Christian a Counselor

**25** *Section Three*: The Big Picture (Watch Counseling Video #2)

**29** *Section Four*: The Eight C's of Biblical Counseling (Watch Counseling Video #3)

**35** *Section Five*: Concepts to Teach (Watch Counseling Video #4)

**45** *Section Six*: Hope (Watch Counseling Video #5)

**31** *Section Seven*: Policy for Counseling Document, Consent to Counsel and Release of Liability, Personal Data Inventory, Case Report Form (Watch Counseling Video #6)

**63** *Section Eight*: Scenario 1 (Watch Counseling Video #7)

**71** *Section Nine*: Scenario 2 (Watch Counseling Video #8)

**77** *Section Ten*: Scenario 3 (Watch Counseling Video #9)

**85** *Section Eleven*: Scenario 4 (Watch Counseling Video #10)

**93** *Section Twelve*: Scenario 5 (Watch Counseling Video #11)

**101** *Section Thirteen*: Scenario 6 (Watch Counseling Video #12)

**109** *Section Fourteen*: What is Biblical Framework Counseling, The Universals of Biblical Framework Counseling, Comparison between Nouthetic and Biblical Framework Counseling

# THE DYNAMICS OF BIBLICAL COUNSELING

**Week One:** What Makes Biblical Counseling Biblical, Qualifications of a Biblical Counselor (Watch Counseling Video #1)

**Week Two:** Every Christian a Counselor

**Week Three:** The Big Picture (Watch Counseling Video #2)

**Week Four:** The Eight C's of Biblical Counseling (Watch Counseling Video #3)

**Week Five:** Concepts to Teach (Watch Counseling Video #4)

**Week Six:** Hope (Watch Counseling Video #5)

**Week Seven:** Policy for Counseling Document, Consent to Counsel and Release of Liability, Personal Data Inventory, Case Report Form (Watch Counseling Video #6)

**Week Eight:** Scenario 1 (Watch Counseling Video #7)

**Week Nine:** Scenario 2 (Watch Counseling Video #8)

**Week Ten:** Scenario 3 (Watch Counseling Video #9)

**Week Eleven:** Scenario 4 (Watch Counseling Video #10)

**Week Twelve:** Scenario 5 (Watch Counseling Video #11)

**Week Thirteen:** Scenario 6 (Watch Counseling Video #12)

**Week Fourteen:** What is Biblical Framework Counseling, The Universals of Biblical Framework Counseling, Comparison between Nouthetic and Biblical Framework Counseling

# THE DYNAMICS OF BIBLICAL COUNSELING

## Section One

## What Makes Biblical Counseling Biblical?

**Key Point**: *Your view of counseling will be determined by your worldview. The more biblical your worldview, the more biblical your counseling. The less biblical your worldview is, the less biblical your counseling will be. Your worldview is determined by those whom you have allowed to teach you. The Bible says, "No student is above his teacher but when fully trained will be like his teacher." (Luke 6:40) You must determine if your view of counseling has been shaped by teaching that is driven by Satan or teaching that is driven by the Son of God! In other words, you must evaluate your model of counseling to determine if it is biblical or unbiblical.*

### Eight Key Questions we can use to evaluate a Model of Counseling to determine if it is biblical or unbiblical?

1. What are the philosophical assumptions about life and God that under gird this model of counseling? (Humanism, Naturalism, Theism, etc.)

2. What is the belief about of the nature of man (model of personality) in this model of counseling?

3. What is the belief about what is wrong with mankind (model of abnormality) in this model of counseling?

4. What is the belief about what makes a healthy/whole human being (model of health) in this model of counseling?

5. What is the method (model of counseling) of leading a person to their view of a healthy/whole human being in this model of counseling?

6. What are the tangible measures (demonstrated effectiveness) to determine success in achieving their goal of a healthy / whole human being?

7. Where does this model contradict, compete with or complement what the Bible says about life, God, the nature or man, or a healthy whole human being?

8. Where does this model contradict, compete with or complement what the Bible says in its methodology and view of success?

## *Three Major Schools of Thoughts in Counseling*

***Psychological Counseling***—combines human observations with human wisdom to construct a system of counsel to help man deal with his problems and issues of life. This type of counseling is generally practiced by non-believers and Christians who accept psychological theories as an avenue to help people.

***Integration Counseling***—combines human observation, human wisdom, and the Bible to construct a system of counsel to help man deal with his problems and issues of life. This is sometimes called "Christian Counseling." This type of counseling is generally practiced by Christians who believe that Bible should be supplemented with psychological theories in order to help people.

***Biblical Counseling***—takes the Bible to construct a system of counsel to help man deal with his non physical or immaterial problems of life. This type of counseling is generally practice by Christians who believe that Bible has all we need to provide solutions to man's non-physical, or immaterial problems as well as what the world calls "psychological" problems. They also believe that the Bible can help man function as God intended in life.

1. Biblical counseling focuses on helping people deal with the heart issues that drive the behavioral issues as explained by God in His Word (James 3:13-4:10, Luke 6:43-45, Matthew 6:19-21, Ezekiel 14:1-11).

2. Biblical counseling focuses on helping people turn from sin in their thoughts, words, actions and relationships as prescribed by God in His Word (Colossians 3:5-9, Ephesians 4:17-22, 1John 1:9, Proverbs 28:13-14).

3. Biblical counseling focuses on helping people walk in Christ's Righteousness in their thoughts, words, actions, and relationships as prescribed by God in His Word (Galatians 5:16-25, Ephesians 4:23-32, Colossians 3:10-25, Romans 12:1-3).

4. Biblical counseling facilitates the process of one becoming like Christ in all aspects of life (Ephesians 4:11-16, Colossians 1:28-29).

5. Biblical Counseling leads a person into truth that comes from God and not human observations and theories that are an antithesis to Scripture (Matthew 28:18-20, 1Timothy 6:3-6, 2Peter 1:16-21).

6. Biblical Counseling leads unbelievers to Christ as it shares with unbelievers their ultimate problem (sin) and their true need salvation (2Corinthians 5:15-21).

7. Biblical Counseling helps individuals in the Body of Christ grow spiritually as it focuses on their real problem—sin—and their solution—Putting off sin and Putting on Righteousness (Ephesians 4:17-32, 2Peter 1:1-10).

8. Biblical Counseling provides the community with God's Solutions to life's immaterial, non physical, or what world calls "psychological" problems (Colossians 1:28-29).

9. Biblical Counseling depends on the sufficiency of Scripture instead of the traditions and theories of man (Colossians 2:8-9, 2Timohty 3:16-17, Psalm 1:1-2, Psalm 19:7-11).

10. Biblical Counseling is rooted and grounded in a worldview that all things are from God, through God, and to God; therefore all things must be evaluated from His perspective (Romans 11:36). Questions such as the following are addressed through God and His Word.

    a. What is the nature of man and what is his relationship to God?
    b. What is man's fundamental problem?
    c. How should we and how do we relate to our fellow human beings?
    d. What values should guide and what values do guide our attitudes and actions?
    e. How can man solve his basic problems?
    f. What specific changes should he make?
    g. Who/what is the agent for such change?
    h. What are the goals of these changes?

11. True Biblical Counseling will demonstrate:

    a. A high View of God in His Character, Nature, Attributes etc.

    b. A high view of the Sufficiency of Scripture.

    c. An accurate anthropology (man is basically evil and in need of salvation/sanctification).

    d. A Biblical understanding of the purpose of the Church.

    e. A Biblical view of Church Leadership.

    f. Insight that is based on Biblical foundations.

    g. Methodologies that are based on Biblical foundations.

    h. Goals that are God-centered instead of man centered.

(Concept #11 adapted from Lance Quinn Senior Pastor of Little Rock Bible Church)

## Qualifications of a Biblical Counselor

1. A Biblical counselor should be one who is guarded and governed by the Holy Spirit thus displaying the fruits of the Holy Spirit in attitudes, values, words and actions (Galatians 6:1).

2. A Biblical Counselor should be one who is aware and honest about his own sinful tendencies and character flaws seeking to deal with them accordingly (Galatians 6:1).

3. A Biblical counselor should be one who ministers by the Word of God and does not use any theories or practices that contradict or violate God's standards (2Timothy 4:1-5).

4. A Biblical counselor should be one who seeks to help others recover from the consequences of poor decisions (Galatians 6:2).

5. A Biblical counselor should be one who seeks to help others confess and repent of sin (Galatians 6:1-2).

6. A Biblical counselor should be one who seeks to help others function in spiritual maturity in all aspects of life (Ephesians 4:11-16).

7. A Biblical counselor should be one who seeks to hold others accountable to stay away from people, places, and products that will lead them into sin (Hebrews 3:12-13).

8. A Biblical counselor should be one who seeks to stimulate others to love and good deeds (Hebrews 10:19-25).

9. A Biblical counselor should be one who is not quarrelsome but kind to all (2Timothy 2:24).

10. A Biblical counselor should be one who is able to teach others the Truth of God's Word (2Timohty 2:24).

11. A Biblical counselor should be one who is able to practice patience when others are mistreating him (2Timohty 2:24).

12. A Biblical counselor should be one who is able to gently correct those who are in opposition to the Truth (2Timothy 2:25).

13. A Biblical counselor should be one who builds up others with his words (Ephesians 4:29).

# THE DYNAMICS OF BIBLICAL COUNSELING

## Section Two

## Every Christian A Counselor

A. God is saving **_souls_** from the power, penalty, and soon the presence of sin (Ephesians 2:1-10, Colossians 1:12-14).

B. God is maturing **_Saints_** into the image of Jesus Christ (2Corinthains 3:18, Romans 8:29-30).

C. God is using the **_Church_** through evangelism to save souls (2Corinthians 5:18-20, Colossians 1:3-6).

D. God is using the **_Church_** through discipleship to mature saints into the image of Christ (Matthew 28:18-20, Ephesians 4:11-15).

E. Biblical Counseling is an **_avenue_** whereby evangelism and discipleship can take place resulting in God using it to save a soul from the power, penalty and soon presence of sin and maturing saints into the image of Jesus Christ. Therefore every Christian should be a counselor!

F. All Biblical Counseling should be built around three key **_objectives:_**

   1. To lead a person into **_salvation_** (2Corinthains 5:11-21).

   2. To lead Christians into **_putting off_** particular sinful habits that keeps them from walking in love toward God and others (Galatians 6:1).

   3. To lead Christians into **_putting on_** loving attitudes and actions towards God and others leading them to become like Christ in all things (Ephesians 4:11-32)

G. There are basic categories of life whereby Biblical Counselors are to lead **_counselees_** through process of putting off particular sinful habits and putting on God-honoring righteous habits.

   1. Biblical Counselors are to help counselees look closely at and work hard on having a **_thought, attitudes, motives/intentions, and desires_** that are pleasing to God as God's Word commands (Romans 12:2-3, 2Corinthian 10:3-5, 1 Corinthians 4:5, Proverbs 16:2, Colossians 3:1-5).

2. Biblical Counselors are to help counselees look closely at work hard on ***communicating*** in ways that are honest and edifying to others as God's Word commands (Ephesians 4:29).

3. Biblical Counselors are to help counselees look closely at and work hard on walking in ***behavior*** that is consistent with Christ's Character as God's Word commands (Ephesians 4:17-32, 5:1-17, Galatians 5:16-26).

4. Biblical Counselors are to help counselees look closely at and work hard on ***relating*** to others in ways that demonstrate the love of Christ as God's Word commands (Romans 12: 9-21, 13:8-12).

5. Biblical Counselors are to help counselees look closely at and work hard on ***serving*** others in ways that will bear their burdens and meet their needs as God's Word commands (Ephesians 4:11-16, 1Peter 4:10-11).

H. There are ***six phases*** that one goes through when genuine change takes place.

1. ***Realization Phase*** - One comes to see truth and understand how it applies to their life (2Timothy 2:24-26).

2. ***Remorse Phase*** - One comes to feel godly sorrow in relation to their sin and desire to make things right with God and others accordingly. (2 Corinthians 7:10).

3. ***Renounce Phase*** - One comes to confess their sin to God and to others when appropriate (Psalm 32:1-11, James 5:16).

4. ***Repentance Phase*** - One comes to turn away from their sin towards God and towards others accordingly (Proverbs 28:13, 2Corinthians 7:10-11).

5. ***Renewal Phase*** - One comes to meditate on the truth so that he/she may learn the new direction by which he/she is to obey God and love others accordingly (Ephesians 4:17-23).

6. ***Replacement Phase*** - One comes to obey God and love others in the area where he/she has disobeyed God and been unloving towards others (Ephesians 4:17-23).

I. Each ***phase of change*** is worked out through ***stages of spiritual growth***. As God is working inside of individuals (Philippians 2:12), they respond accordingly (Philippians 2:13). Here is an example of how it works (2Timothy 3:16-17):

1. **<u>Teaching Stage</u>**: The Holy Spirit guides, convicts and enlightens your mind through the Word of God, the Body of Christ, circumstances, and prayer (John 16:8-13, 1Corinthians 2:9-12, Hebrews 4:12, 1John 4:4-6, 1Peter 4:12-13, Romans 8:26-27). (Realization Phase occurs as a result.)

2. **<u>Conviction Stage</u>**: God begins to focus your attention in particular areas of life convincing you that change is necessary. (Phil. 3:14-15, 2Cor. 7:10-11). (Realization Phase and Remorse Phase occurs as a result.)

3. **<u>Correction Stage</u>**: You make a decision to abandon a sin issue and begin a new thought, word, or action trusting God's power to make things function accordingly (2Corinthians 7:10-11, Proverbs 28:13-14). (Renounce Phase and Repentance Phase occurs as a result.)

4. **<u>Training Stage</u>**: As you are responding to God's conviction you are seeking to put to practice what God has commanded in His Word. By the power of God you are walking in harmony with God in areas where you were once disobedient. You are experiencing victory: a deeper fellowship with God and with others (2Peter 1:1-11, Proverbs 12:13, 24:16, John 8:31-32, Luke 8:4-18, Ephesians 4:11-13, 1John 3:1-3). (Renewal Phase and Replacement Phase occurs as a result.)

J. There are several key concepts to teach within the counseling process to help counselees through each phase and stage of change.

1. ***<u>The Gospel</u>*** – The Person and work of Jesus Christ for sins and salvation of mankind.

2. ***<u>What I Can and Cannot Control</u>***- We cannot control people and outcome of situations, we can control our own thoughts, motives, desires, words, will; therefore, our choices reveal both our love for God and love for others or our selfish ambition with people and circumstances.

3. ***<u>The Two Choice in Life</u>***- There are only two choices in life; We are either God-centered or self-centered; Our choices reveal our thoughts; Our thoughts are motivated by indwelling sin or by the Holy Spirit; When our thoughts are motived by indwelling sin we worship our desires turning them into lusts of our lives and we look to people, places, products, perspectives to satisfy them turning them into idols we use to satisfy our lustful desires.

4. ***<u>Idolatrous Lust</u>***- Something you bow down to that you believe will bring you what you truly treasure while making what you truly treasure something you bow down to in place of the living God. The ***<u>avenues</u>*** we pursue and bow down to in the form of worship (Idols) along with these ***<u>treasures</u>*** we bow down to in the form of worship (Lusts) make up the idolatrous lust in our lives.

5. ***The Cycle of Relationships*** - When we walk in pride we relate to people according to our picture, preferences, and presumptions leading to pain in our hearts and the practice of treating people in unloving ways; When we walk in humility we relate to people according to their position before God and others, the priority of God for others and the precept of God for others resulting in peace in our hearts and the practice of love towards others.

6. ***The Four Kinds of Human Relationships*** - Understanding what it means to be open and unloving, closed and loving, open and loving and closed and unloving.

7. ***Biblical View of Love*** - Understanding what it means to love according to 1 Corinthians 13:1-8.

8. ***Living by Purpose*** - Understanding and developing a Christ-Centered life.

9. ***Conflict Resolution*** - Understanding why conflict exist and how to resolve it from addressing heart issues instead of just dealing with behavior.

10. ***The Biblical Framework*** - Understanding what happens to man in his heart when he chooses to sin and when he chooses to live righteously.

11. ***Immaterial Pain Vs Material Pain*** – Understanding that all pain is not the same. Some pain is the result of issues going in within the immaterial heart of man (Soul/Spirit). Some pain is the result of material issues (physical body). Some pain in the physical body happens as a result of pain of the immaterial heart. Deal with physical pain according to medication and all that the medical world can provide. Deal with immaterial pain according to the Messiah and all He has to provide. Do not confuse the two.

K. There are *six* key categories of homework that can be given to guide counselees into the process of change according to each phase and stage. This is to lead them into escaping the corruption of their flesh, the world and the devil unto spiritual maturity in Jesus Christ:

1. ***Hope Homework*** – projects, activities and reading assignments given to help people gain a true hope in Christ in accordance to the problems they are facing (Used in all stages of spiritual growth)

2. ***Doctrinal Homework*** – projects, activities, and reading assignments given to help people gain a solid theological understanding of their problems so that they can deal with them properly (Used to lead people into the Teaching Stage of spiritual growth)

3. *__Awareness Homework__* – projects, activities, and reading assignments given to help people become aware of their own sinfulness in the problem so that they can stop deceiving themselves about the problem they are facing and own up to it accordingly (Used to lead people into the Conviction Stage of spiritual growth)

4. *__Embracing God Homework__* – projects, activities, and reading assignments given to help people to connect with God according to a particular characteristic of God that relates to their problem or sin (Used to lead people into the Correction and Training Stage of spiritual growth)

5. *__Action Oriented Homework__* – projects and activities that lead people to put off particular sinful thoughts, desires, conversations, behavior, and lifestyle and to put on particular godly thoughts, desires conversations, behavior, and lifestyle according to the situation or problem (Used to lead people into the Correction and Training Stage of Spiritual growth)

6. *__Relational Oriented Homework__* – projects and activities that lead people to put off unloving relational patterns and move them to relate in open and loving relational patterns towards others within the situation or problem and abroad (Used to lead people into the Correction and Training Stage of spiritual growth)

(Portions of this information was adapted from *Instruments in a Redeemer's Hand* by Paul Tripp)

L. As a counselor determines the category of homework to be given, he can use various ***methods*** of implementation to help move counselees through each phase and stage resulting in escaping the corruption of their flesh, the world and the devil unto spiritual maturity in Jesus Christ. Some of those methods of implementation are:

1. *__Scripture reading__* – leading the counselee into seeing and discovering the reality of God's Word in
accordance to their problem; to lead them into a consistent pattern of reading and studying God's Word to understand the nature of it and to live by the content in it in order that they may know God intimately and to be useful to Him practically (Concept adapted from Randy Patten)

2. *__Literature reading__* – leading the counselee into reading various biblical literature that shows them how to evaluate and address the problem from God's standpoint in a comprehensive manner so that they may turn from it and walk in obedience to God accordingly (Concept adapted from Randy Patten)

3. *__Scripture Memorization__* – leading the counselee into memorizing Scripture so that they may be transformed in their thinking and turn away from sin unto living as God has commanded (Concept adapted from Randy Patten)

4. _**Prayer**_ – leading the counselee into the process of prayer so they may learn how to communicate with God in a way that will lead them into genuine fellowship with God; so they my learn how to make request for others and themselves in an appropriate manner (Concept adapted from Randy Patten)

5. _**Projects**_ – activities that lead the counselee into stopping some thought, word or action or leading them into starting some thought, word, or action in relation to God, others, self or circumstances as it relates to the issues brought up in the counseling sessions (Concept adapted from Randy Patten)

6. _**Log Lists/Journals**_ – having the counselee to write down specific thoughts, behaviors, actions or words to evaluate where change has taken place or to see where change needs to take place

7. _**Church Participation**_ – leading the counselee into:

   - _**Membership**_ – the counselee would be lead to join a local church that they may experience love and enjoy the blessings of God-honoring relationships.

   - _**Maturity**_ – the counselee would be lead to get involved in discipleship courses in a local Church that would lead them into loving God, loving others on a consistent basis and living a life that reflects the character of Christ

   - _**Magnification**_ – the counselee would be led to come to appreciate value and adore the character of God through heart-felt genuine worship of Him in a local Church.

   - _**Ministry**_ – the counselee would be led to join a ministry where they can develop in bearing burdens and meeting needs according to the various relationships they will develop through the local Church

   - _**Missions**_ – the counselee would be led into supporting a local Church in sharing and defending the Christian faith

M. Overall, Biblical Counselors are to lead _**counselees**_ into:

1. Gaining a biblical understanding of God and submitting to God's will accordingly.

2. Gaining a biblical understanding of themselves and submitting to God's will accordingly.

3. Gaining a biblical understanding of others and submitting to God's will accordingly.

4. Gaining a biblical understanding of life's situations and circumstances and submitting to God's will accordingly.

N. There are four basic ***kinds of counselees*** you may run into when involved in biblical counseling:

1. Those that ***lack knowledge*** on what to do in the situation. (Don't know what to do in the situation.)

2. Those that ***have knowledge*** but ***lack skill*** on how to apply the knowledge to their situation. (Know what to do but do not know how to do it in relation to the situation.)

3. Those that ***have knowledge*** and ***have skill*** on how to apply the knowledge to their situation but refuse to apply what they know to the situation. (Know what to do and how to do it but refuse to do what they know in the situation.)

4. Those that ***lack knowledge*** and ***lack skill*** on how to apply the knowledge to their situation and are not interested in gaining either. (Don't know what to do in the situation or how to do it in the situation and are not interested in learning either.) *(Adapted from the various teachings of Jay Adams)*

O. A Counselee is ready to be released or graduated from counseling when:

1. The counselee understands their problem from a biblical perspective.

2. The counselee understands the biblical solutions to their problem.

3. The counselee consistently applies the principles to address their problems to put off sin and to put on what is right resulting in living out in practice what they have learned.

P. Given these factors, true biblical counseling (which in essence is evangelism and discipleship) will help people through each phase, stage, and categories of life by the practice of 7 key procedures (1Thessalonians 5:14-24):

1. **Commend Submission (1 Thessalonians 5:11). (Concept adapted from David Powlison)**
   A. Congratulate the person in areas they are seeking to do right thing in relation to the situation.
   B. Complement the person in areas they refused to do the wrong thing in relation to the situation.

2. **Console suffering (Romans 12:15)**
   A. Connect with the pain of the sufferer.
   B. Consider the peace God can bring to the sufferer.

3. **Confront sin (Galatians 6:1).**
   A. Call out sin with compassion.
   B. Challenge sin with care.

4. **Characterize Sovereign (Colossians 1:28-29). (Concept adapted from David Powlison)**
   A. Discuss the aspects of God's character that would be appropriate to discuss in relation to the situation.
   B. Dialogue about how those aspects of God's character can be used for warning and teaching the person accordingly in relation to the situation.

5. **Communicate salvation (Matthew 28:18-20).**
   A. Present the Gospel of Jesus Christ.
   B. Provide the guidance into receiving the Gospel of Jesus Christ.

6. **Clarify sanctification (Matthew 28:18-20).**
   A. Teach the specific sins that need to be put off and how to do it through the Word of God.
   B. Tutor the specific solutions that need to be put on in place of the specific sins that demonstrate love for God and love for others through the Word of God.

7. **Celebrate summation (Philippians 3:13-21).**
   A. Promote the promise of the return of Jesus Christ.
   B. Proclaim the prizes that come with the return of Jesus Christ.

| The Areas of Change | The Phases of Change | The Stages of Spiritual Growth | Concepts to Teach in the Biblical counseling Sessions | The Homework to help implement Change | The Methods to help implement the homework | The Examples of Implementation of activities | Seven Key Procedures |
|---|---|---|---|---|---|---|---|
| Thought (Idea) | Realize truth | Teaching Stage- Realize truth | The Gospel/What I Can and Cannot Control | Hope Homework | Scripture Reading | Reading particular Books of the Bible that connect to your issues | Commend Submission |
| Attitude (Belief System that results from a pattern of Ideas) | Realize and Remorse over our Sin in connection with truth | Conviction Stage- Realize and Remorse over our sin in connection with truth | The Two Choices Concept | Theological Homework | Literature Reading | Reading literature that addresses your issues | Console Suffering |
| Motives or Intentions/Desires | Renounce our Sin | Correction Stage- Renounce our Sin; Repent of our Sin | Idolatrous Lust/ The Four Kinds of Human Relationships | Awareness Homework | Scripture Memorization | Memorizing and Meditating on Scripture/ Biblical Concepts according to your issues | Confront Sin |
| Communicational Patterns | Repent of our Sin | Training Stage- Renew our minds; Replace our Sin with the right thing to do in the areas change | Biblical View of Love/Living by Purpose | Embracing God Homework | Prayer | Writing out Log list, or journals to evaluate yourself or your progress | Characterize Sovereign |
| Behavioral and Relational Patterns | Renew our Minds | | Conflict Resolution | Action Oriented Homework | Projects | Communicating certain things to God or people on a regular basis | Communicate Salvation |
| Service for God and Others | Replace our Sin with the right thing to do in the areas of change | | Biblical Framework | Relation Oriented Homework | Log List/ Journals/ Church Participation | Practicing certain attitudes, actions or behaviors towards God, others, and in situations/ Getting involved in particular aspects of Church life to enhance growth in Christ | Clarify Sanctification/ Celebrate Summation |

# The Three Basic Responses to People and Circumstances

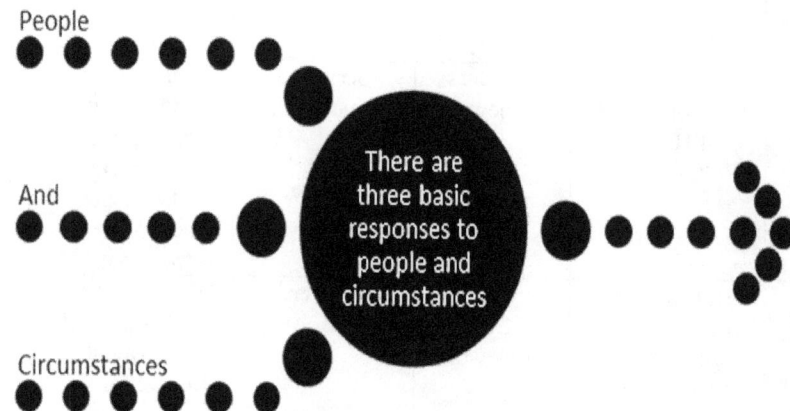

# Four Key Issues Revealed in Our Responses to People and Circumstances

```
People ●●●●●●                                    ┌─────────────────────────────┐
                                                 │ Expectaions and desires of   │
                                                 │ Life that have become the    │
                                                 │ central focus of our         │
                                                 │ attenation above love for    │
                                                 │ God and love for others      │
                                                 └─────────────────────────────┘

                                                 ┌─────────────────────────────┐
                                                 │ Thoughts, motives, desires,  │
                                                 │ communiacation patterns,     │
                                                 │ behavior patterns,           │
                                                 │ relationial patterns,        │
                                                 │ serving patterns that are    │
                                                 │ displeasing to God and that  │
                                                 │ God wants changed for His    │
                    ┌───────────────┐            │ Glory, the good of others    │
                    │   What is     │            │ and our good.                │
And ●●●●●●          │  revealed in  │ ●●●●●●     └─────────────────────────────┘
                    │ our responses │
                    │ to people and │            ┌─────────────────────────────┐
                    │ circumstances │            │ Thoughts, motives, desires,  │
                    └───────────────┘            │ communiacation patterns,     │
                                                 │ behavior patterns,           │
                                                 │ relationial patterns,        │
                                                 │ serving patterns that are    │
                                                 │ pleasing to God and are      │
                                                 │ Glorifying God, good to      │
                                                 │ others and our own good      │
Circumstances ●●●●●●                             └─────────────────────────────┘

                                                 ┌─────────────────────────────┐
                                                 │ The reality that one does    │
                                                 │ not have a genuine           │
                                                 │ relationship with God and is │
                                                 │ need of deliverance from the │
                                                 │ penatly and power of sin     │
                                                 │ unto a new and right         │
                                                 │ relationship with God.       │
                                                 └─────────────────────────────┘
```

# WHAT I CANNOT AND CAN CONTROL

We cannot control people or the outcome of situations (Ecclesiastes 3:1-11, 7:13-14, 9:1-2.) We can only control our own thoughts, emotions, desires, words, and actions. (Romans 12:2-3, Proverbs 16:32, Psalm 37:4, Ephesians 4:29, 22-24) Therefore, we need to evaluate and take responsibility for how we are responding to people and the outcome of situations. (Galatians 6:7-8, 5:16-25) We need to evaluate what is motivating us with people and the outcome of situations. (James 1:13-14, 3:13-16, 4:1-3). Are we motivated by love for God above our selfish desires? Or, are we motivated by our selfish desires above love for God? (1John 2:15-16, James 4:4, James 3:16)

# Looking at Some Central Heart Issues

**Pride**
- Mind Set on Self; Self-Centeredness
- Life revolves around what is important to you above what is important to God. When what God says contradicts what you think, you allow what you think to be the perspective you hold above what God says. Interpret the Scripture to fit your agenda.

**Lust**
- Consumed with what you treasure above loving God and loving others. Willing to sin to get this treasure and to sin when cannot recieve this treasure. This treasure in essence has become an all consuming desire that you allow to become the center of your attention above loving God and loving others.

**Idolatry**
- Will use- People, Places, Products, or Perspectives as means to obtain or to satisfy the lust of one's life; They are placed above God to satisfy the lustful desires you treasure above loving God and lvoing others. They are the means to your lustful end.

**Worry-**
disturbing or disquieting thoughts of the mind as one is consumed with the possibility of loosing or not recieving something they treausre

**Anger-**
to have ungodly attitudes, words, or actions as a result of some perceived need, desires, personal preferecence, or standard not being met, by someone or in circumstances

**Depression-**
enslaving thought, mood, or feeling of unhappiness which becomes the reason people give for not functioning as they should

As you walk in pride, you will be consumed with lust. As you are consumed with lust you will seek idols to satisfy your lustful desires. When the idols seemingly are not going to follow through your expectation to satisfy your lustful desires you may begin to worry. When the idols do not follow through on your expectation to satisfy your lustful desires you may fall into anger. All of this worry and anger could possibly lead you to depression. As you listen and talk with people evaluate how you are responding to other people and circumstances. Listen to the dominating topics of conversation to determine what you tend to treasure, dislike, worry about and get angry about. Learn the people, places, products, and perspectives you tend to discuss the most and why. Listen to see if your primary conversations are driven by discussions of yourself or others things more important than yourself. Identify who or what tends to lead you to react in happiness or sadness.

# Direction and Result of Addressing Some Central Heart Issues

### Humility
- Mind set on Jesus Christ; God-Centeredness; Submission to God;
- Embracing and submitting to one's roles and responsibilities in life according to God's Word.
- Life revolves around what is important to God above your desires that have become sinful and have led you into sin. When your sin-focused desires contradict what God commands you allow what God commands to be the perspective you submit to above your sin-focused desires. You pursue God and find more pleasure in that above your sin-focused desires.

### Love For God
- Consumed with following the commands of God. You are devoted to doing what God says in all aspects of life. Because you want to know Jesus Christ intimately, be like Jesus Christ, and be useful to Jesus Christ, you are willing and wanting to follow the commands of God knowing obedience leads to knowing, becoming like and being useful to Jesus Christ. You focus on doing what God says in your thoughts, motives, desires, words, actions & way of life. Because God first loved you, you seek to love Him by your submission to Him accordingly in all aspects of life.

### Love For Others
- Consumed with treating people with the highest level of what is called appropriate by Scripture unconditionally. Seeking the highest good of others unconditionally. Taking the characteristics of 1 Corinthians 13:4-8 and applying them accordingly to all unconditionally.
- Serving others unconditionally with the spiritual gifts God has given you. You become an ambassador to unbelievers and a builder of believers unconditionally.

### Embracing God-
Entrusting one's self to God according to the specific characteristics of God as one encounters all aspects of life.

### Accepting What God Allows-
Enduring the difficult, disappointing and down times of life knowing God is working out His ultimate good in your life through them; Enjoying the delightful times of life knowing God has granted them for your enjoyment and development as well; Submitting to your roles and responsibilities during the good and bad times because of your commitment to and confidence in God. Living by your commitment to God, and confidence in God above your mood of the moment.

### Peace of God
Tranquility of the heart as a result of embracing God and accepting what God allows in one's life. Calmness of soul regardless of the situation because of one's surrender to and submission to God accordingly.

As you walk in humility, you will be preoccupied with love for God. As you are preoccupied with love for God you will develop in genuine love for others. As you walk in love for God and love for others you will develop in embracing God and accepting what God allows as you live by your trust in the person, plans, precepts and promises of God. Living this way involves living by your commitment to God and confidence in God above your mood of the moment. As you develop in living by your commitment to God and confidence in God, you will experience the peace of God in your life on a consistent basis in the good and bad of life. Overall, as you develop in living by humility, love for God and others, embracing God, and accepting what God allows, you will not only experience the peace of God consistently, but you will find yourself turning away from a life reduced to making God, people and circumstances the help to or the complaint against you accomplishing your personal ambitions. Living a life where you make God, people and circumstances the help to or the complaint against you accomplishing your personal ambitions reveal the pride, lust, idolatry, worry, or anger in your life which can lead to depression in your life. Evaluate your life and see where you stand. Identify where you are lacking in humility, in love for God and others, in embracing God, in accepting what God allows and in the peace of God. Move into the process of remorse over your sin accordingly, renouncing of your sin accordingly, repenting of your sin accordingly, renewing your mind in the truth of humility, love for God and others, embracing God, accepting what God allows, and the peace of God. Replace the pride, lust, idolatry, worry, anger, (and all other sins discovered) which can lead to depression with humility, love for God and others, embracing God, accepting what God allows, which will result in the peace of God accordingly on consistent basis in the good and bad of life. You will see a difference in your life when you start living for God and stop living for yourself. People and circumstances will be handled by God's agenda. You will find that life is more satisfying and productive as you live to please God instead of seeking to use God, people or circumstances to accomplish what is and has been more important to you above your allegiance to and obedience to God. You will find that life is more satisfying and productive as you live to please God instead of being worried or angry with God, people, or circumstances as a result of them falling short of providing what is and has been more important to you above your allegiance to and obedience to God.

# THE DYNAMICS OF BIBLICAL COUNSELING

## Section Three

## BIG PICTURE FOR BIBLICAL COUNSELING

1. There are only two central commands that sum up all commands:
   A. Love God
   B. Love Others

2. Man's basic problem is a lack of love of God or a lack of love of others which is what sin is: If you love me you will keep my commandments/Love your neighbor as yourself. To disobey God is to sin. To sin is to lack love for God and to lack love for others.

3. Man's lack of love for God and others shows up in five places:
   A. C1. Thoughts, motives, desire
   B. C2. Communicating
   C. C3. Behavior/ manner of life/ conduct/ commitments
   D. C4. Relating to others
   E. C5. Serving others

4. We will see a lack of love for God or others in areas C1- through C5 as we observe people's actions, reactions or responses to other people and circumstances.

5. Our mission is to help people see the lack of love for God or others in areas C1-C5 and to help move them from a lack of love for God and others to walking in love for God and others.

6. The root lack of love will be found in C1.

7. The fruit lack of love will be found in C2-C5.

8. We will help people understand how C1 is driving C2-C5.

9. We will then lead them to walk in love for God and others in C1-C5.

10. The tools we have to do this are the worksheets and homework assignment we give.

11. Therefore as we observe people's actions, reactions or responses to other people and circumstances or listen to them talk about these issues we should listen, identify and document our observations on 7 basic levels:

    a. Level 1 Listen, identify and document the C1-C5 Issues being presented or discussed
    b. Level 2 Listen, identify and document what they can and cannot control according to the issues presented or discussed
    c. Level 3 Listen, identify and document the person(s) actions, reactions, or responses to other people and circumstances being presented or discussed
    d. Level 4 Listen, identify, and document where their actions, reactions, or responses fit on the Biblical Framework
    e. Level 5 Listen, identify and document the belief systems, agendas, and desires being revealed from their actions, reactions, or responses being presented or discussed
    f. Level 6 Listen, identify and document the pride, lust, and idols, being revealed from their actions, reactions, or responses being presented or discussed
    g. Level 7 Listen, identify and document the C2-C5 issues that are the by-products of the C1 issues

12. We will lead them to see and understand these things through the worksheets and homework we will give them.

13. We will lead them to renounce, repent, and replace these things with Love for God and love for others through the worksheets and homework we will give them.

14. We will lead them to do all of this according to the phases and stages of change the person is in accordingly.

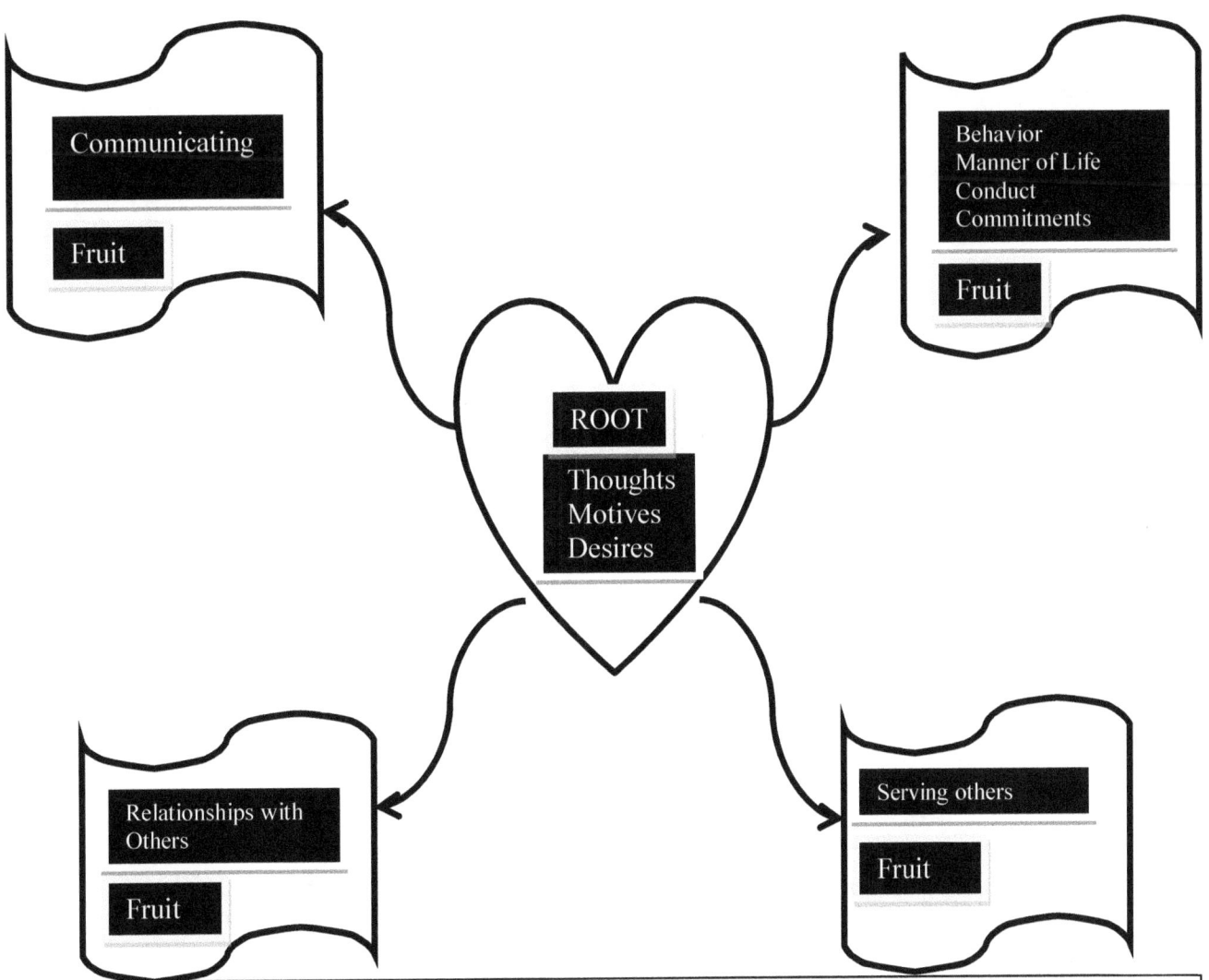

In summary, people who come in for counseling are bringing in a lot of data to us which are the fruit of their root sin. Their Lack of Love for God and others is sinful.

Lack of Love for God:
John 14:15 "If you love Me, you will keep My commands."

Lack of Love for Others:
Mark 12:31 "The second is, Love your neighbor as yourself. There is no other command greater than these."

When gathering data, we must look beyond the "fruit" sin and stay attentive to their speech for the "root" sin. Keep the "root" in your mind as they are communicating to you.
Luke 6:45 "A good man brings good things out of the good stored up in his heart, and an evil man brings evil things out of the evil stored up in his heart. For the mouth speaks what the heart is full of."

Do not get caught up in the "fruit" "drama" but instead ask good questions to search for the root. "What motivated you to do that?" "What were you desiring at that moment?" and so forth. If you stay in the "fruit" of the issues…you will get caught up in the "leaves" therefore blinding you to see the "root."

**(Graphics and summary created by Keith and Jujuan Bowen)**

# The Dynamics of Biblical Counseling

## Section Four

## The 8 "C"s of Biblical Counseling

1. **<u>Connect</u>** with the counselee in the first part of the counseling session.

   A. Ask your counselee questions that will help you to get to know them better.

   B. Identify areas of common interest and share those with the counselee.

   C. Share things about yourself that you think will lead your counselee to be comfortable with you. (Proverbs 16:24))

2. **<u>Console</u>** the Counselee during the counseling session.

   A. Give words of hope and encouragement to assure the counselee that God has solutions to their problem.

   B. Provide comfort as the counselee shares their problems and concerns.

   C. Be compassionate and patient as your counselee shares their heart with you.

3. **<u>Collect</u>** data from the Counselee in regards to their problems and concerns.

   A. Find out what is happening or has happened to the person.

   B. Identify what they cannot control, what they can control, the motives (God-centered or self-centered) that are being revealed in their choices or responses to the people/circumstances accordingly.

   C. Find out how they are responding in thoughts, words, behavior, lifestyle, relational patterns to what is happening or has happened (neutral, unloving, loving responses).

   D. Identify time frame of responses to people, places, and events in accordance to what is happening or has happened.

   E. Find out what they want that they cannot control getting and what they are getting they do not want.

   F. Identify areas of pride, idolatrous lust, worry, anger, fear, depression.

G. Find out what the person's perceptions, preferences, pains, passions are in connection to what is happening or has happened.

H. Find out how the person has dealt with or is dealing with sin towards God and others.

I. Look for any and all unloving thoughts, words, and actions.

4. ***Categorize*** data from the Counselee into Biblical terms and perspectives as you are thinking through Biblical solutions.

   A. Where there is a biblical term or interpretation for the data use it in place of psychological terms so that those issues may be dealt with accordingly.

   B. Identify and interpret data that is an expression of apparently uncaused fleeing as such when you are collecting the data. (See the book ***The Heart of Man and the Mental Disorders*** by Rich Thomson for insight into this.)

   C. Identify and interpret data that is an expression of apparently uncaused fear as such when you are collecting the data. (See the book ***The Heart of Man and the Mental Disorders*** by Rich Thomson for insight into this.)

   D. Identify and interpret data that is an expression of a sense of guilt as such when you are collecting the data. (See the book ***The Heart of Man and the Mental Disorders*** by Rich Thomson for insight into this.)

   E. Identify and interpret first level and second level sins, root sins and fruit sins as such when you are collecting the data. (See the book ***The Heart of Man and the Mental Disorders*** by Rich Thomson for insight into this.)

   F. Identify and interpret what a person can and cannot control in their situation past, present, future as you are collecting the data.

   G. Identify and interpret their conduct, character, and conversation according to Biblical perspectives.

5. **Communicate** to Counselee what the Bible defines as the source and the symptoms of the problems in Biblical terms and ***clarify*** what the Biblical solutions are to those problems.

   A. Explain the concept of the Gospel.

   B. Explain the concept of What I Cannot and Can Control.

   C. Explain the concept of the Biblical Framework.

   D. Explain the concept of The Point of Choice.

E. Explain the concept of Pride.

F. Explain the concept of Idolatrous Lust.

G. Explain the concepts of Worry, Anger, Fear.

H. Explain the concept of the Cycle of Relationships.

I. Explain the concept of four kinds of human relationships.

J. Explain the concept of Love for God and others.

K. Explain the concept of progressive sanctification.

L. Explain the concept of confession, repentance, and replacement.

M. Explain the material and immaterial issues of man.

N. Explain the concept of guilt and the standards of the conscience.

O. Explain the fear of man, anxiety and the solutions.

P. Explain the concept of embracing God according to who He is.

Q. Explain the concept of being controlled by the Holy Spirit.

**6.** ***Challenge*** the Counselee to a commitment to confess, repent, and replace sin with love for God and others.

A. Ask the counselee if they are willing to do the hard work of confessing, repenting, radically amputating and replacing sin to walk in love for God and others.

B. Explain to the counselee the importance of being a doer of the Word and not just a hearer of the Word.

C. Explain what kind of commitment it will take to make the appropriate changes to resolve the problem and become Godly in the situation.

7. **Construct** homework for the counselee to apply to their lives that will lead them into confession, repentance and replacement of sin with love for God and others.

   A. *Hope Homework* – projects, activities and reading assignments given to help people gain a true hope in Christ in accordance to the problems they are facing.

   B. *Doctrinal Homework* – projects, activities, and reading assignments given to help people gain a solid theological understanding of their problems so that they can deal with them properly.

   C. *Awareness Homework* – projects, activities, and reading assignments given to help people become aware of their own sinfulness in the problem so that they can stop deceiving themselves about the problem they are facing and own up to it accordingly.

   D. *Embracing God Homework* – projects, activities, and reading assignments given to help people to connect with God according to a particular characteristic of God that relates to their problem or sin.

   E. *Action Oriented Homework* – projects and activities that lead people to put off particular sinful thoughts, desires, conversations, behavior, and lifestyle and to put on particular godly thoughts, desires, conversations, behavior, and lifestyle that according to the situation or problem.

   F. *Relational Orientated Homework* – projects and activities that lead people to put off unloving relational patterns and move them to relate in open and loving relational patterns towards others within the situation or problem and abroad. (Portions of this information was adapted from *Instruments in a Redeemer's Hand* by Paul Tripp)

8. **Conjoin** the counselee to the Body of Christ according to where they need it.

   A. *Membership* – the counselee would be lead to join a local church that they may experience love and enjoy the blessings of God-honoring relationships.

   B. *Maturity* – the counselee would be lead to get involved in discipleship courses in a local Church that would lead them into loving God, loving others on a consistent basis and living a life that reflects the character of Christ

   C. *Magnification* – the counselee would be led to come to appreciate value and adore the character of God through heart-felt genuine worship of Him in a local Church.

D. ***Ministry*** – the counselee would be led to join a ministry where they can develop in bearing burdens and meeting needs according to the various relationships they will develop through the local Church

E. ***Missions*** – the counselee would be led into supporting a local Church in sharing and defending the Christian faith

# The Dynamics of Biblical Counseling

## Section Five

## Key Concepts to Teach Your Counselee in order to Lead Him into Biblical Change

| **Concept 1 – The Gospel of Jesus Christ** | |
|---|---|
| <ul><li>Teach who Jesus Christ is.</li><li>Teach the doctrine of salvation</li></ul> | <ul><li>Teach the way of salvation</li><li>Teach the evidence that validates one has received salvation</li></ul><br>(Bullet points adapted from Randall D. Westerberg from a paper "The Lack of Assurance of Salvation"; Doctorate of Ministry Paper for Southern Baptist Theological Seminary) |
| **Concept 2 – Understanding the Difference Between Faith That Works And Working For Salvation** | |
| <ul><li>Explain Paul's Theology of Faith.</li><li>Explain James' Theology of Faith</li></ul> | <ul><li>Show how Paul and James are explaining different sides of the faith in Jesus Christ.</li><li>Explain how one cannot work for their salvation</li></ul> |
| **Concept 3 – True Faith in the Gospel Vs Intellectual Awareness of the Gospel** | |
| <ul><li>Explain how intellectual assent to the person and work of Christ is not trust in Jesus Christ.</li><li>Explain how genuine faith in the person and work of Jesus Christ goes beyond intellectual assent to putting trust in what one understands.</li></ul> | <ul><li>Show the dangers of intellectual assent.</li><li>Show the benefits of genuine faith in Jesus Christ.</li></ul> |
| **Concept 4 – From Salvation to Sanctification to Satisfaction** | |
| <ul><li>Explain how we were saved from the penalty, power, and soon presence of sin.</li><li>Explain how we are saved unto sanctification into the image of Jesus Christ.</li></ul> | <ul><li>Explain how sanctification will lead to satisfaction as we obey God.</li><li>Explain how Psalm 16:11 applies to the salvation, sanctification, and satisfaction experience.</li></ul> |

## Concept 5 – Spiritual Deception

- Teach people the danger of practicing religion.
- Teach people how easy it is to be deceived into thinking they are Christians due to some acts of ministry service when actually they are not.

- Help people examine themselves to see if they are deceived about being a Christian.
- Lead them into faith if they have been deceived.

## Concept 6 – Spiritual Amnesia

- Explain how some Christians have forgotten the purpose of their salvation.
- Explain how the light of the world has dimmed their eyes to the light of God.

- Teach them the way of repentance.
- Teach the way of sanctification.

## Concept 7 – Three Basic Responses to People and Circumstances

- We can have a neutral response- disappointed or grief; something that is not regarded as wrong or right before God hence neutral ( i.e. Job when he suffered great loss).
- We can have an unloving response- reacting in ways the Bible defines as sin ( i.e. Saul's response to David).

- We can have a loving response – reacting in ways the Bible would define as right in the sight of God ( i.e. Stephens response while being stoned as read in the book of Acts).

## Concept 8 – Four Key Issues Revealed In Our Responses to People And Circumstances

- Expectations or desires that have become the central focus of one's life.
- Unloving responses – reacting in ways the Bible defines as sin.

- Loving responses- reacting in ways the Bible would define as right in the sight of God.
- The reality that one is not a Christian.

## Concept 9 – What I Cannot and Can Control

- Teach the person to distinguish between what he/she is concerned about and what he is responsible for.
- Help the person understand how not making the distinction can create complications resulting in him/her negating his/her responsibilities by being consumed with what he is concerned about but cannot control.
- Help the person understand that he cannot control what people think, say, or do.
- Help the person understand that he cannot control the outcome of events.

- Teach the person that he can control what he thinks, says, does.
- Help the person understand that he is motivated either by selfish desires or love for God in relation to people and situations.
- Help the person understand that the condition of his life is a by-product of heart choices not the actions of others or circumstances in life.

## Concept 10 – The Point of Choice

- Teach the person that he is either God-centered or self-centered.
- Teach the person that his choices are driven by his/her thoughts.
- Teach the person that at the core of his thoughts is either the love of self and the love of pleasure or the love of God and the love of others.

- Help the person understand that if he is consumed with the love of pleasure and the love of self he may create idols and lust in his heart and bring destruction to his life as a result.
- Teach him the steps to turn from this sin and all other sinful ways and turn to God.

## Concept 11 – The Biblical Framework

- Help him understand that our ambition in life is to please God.
- Help him understand that God has given us two basic commandments to please Him (Love God and Love His Neighbor).
- Teach him that God has set up consequences within our hearts to happen when we don't walk in love for God and love for others.
- Teach him that God has set up consequences within our hearts to happen when we walk in love for God and love for others.

- Help him learn and understand the principle and picture of a sense of guilt, apparently uncaused fear, and apparently uncaused fleeing as the consequences of not walking in love for God and others.
- Help him learn and understand the principle and picture of the peace of God, confidence before God and drawing near to God as the consequences of walking in love for God and others.
- Help him learn and understand the process of moving from a lack of love for God and others to love for God and others.

## Concept 12 – Pride

- Explain that pride is ultimately a self-centered way of living.
- Give examples of pride.

- Help the person learn how pride operates in their life.
- Lead the person to repent of pride.

## Concept 13 – Idolatrous Lust

- Teach the concept of idols.
- Give examples of idols.
- Teach the concept of lust.
- Give examples of lust.

- Explain the term Idolatrous Lust accordingly
- Give demonstrations of how Idols are used to gain lustful desires of one's heart.
- Help the person identify the idolatrous lusts of his heart.
- Lead the person to repentance and embracing God accordingly.

## Concept 14 – Emotions

- Define emotions from the Latin- which means to stir up one to actions.
- Explain and demonstrate how emotions come from thoughts of the mind and brain.

- Explain and demonstrate how emotions operate.
- Help individuals connect the teaching to their lives accordingly.

## Concept 15 – Anger

- Define anger- a disposition of the mind that entertains antagonism towards others resulting in various emotions and actions.
- Help people see that anger is an attitude that moves into emotions and then expresses itself in various actions.

- Lead people into understanding that the driving force behind anger are the desires that have become demands that are not being satisfied resulting in one responding in anger to unmet desires that have become demands..
- Lead people to repent and embrace God accordingly.

## Concept 16 – Worry

- Define worry- the fear of not getting something you want or need, the fear losing something you want or need, or the fear of getting something you don't want or need as a result of being consumed and controlled by these things that are very important to you from this world below and in this world below.
- Help people see that worry is an attitude that moves into emotions causing one to be negatively preoccupied with what may or may not happen

- Lead people into understanding that the driving force behind worry are the desires that have become demands that one has the potential to loose or gain resulting in one responding in worry to the future potential.
- Lead people to repent and embrace God accordingly.

## Concept 17 – Kinds of Sorrow

- Teach and explain common sorrow- a sadness of the soul due to one experiencing the disappointments of life, the difficulties of life, or the death of a loved one.
- Teach and explain chosen sorrow- a sadness of the soul created by one grumbling or complaining about their circumstances.
- Teach and explain conscience sorrow- a sadness of soul as a result one's conscience bringing about guilt due to some act(s) of sin in one's life.

- Teach and explain casualty sorrow- a sadness of soul as result of regret over the consequences of sin choices ultimately leading one to death because of a lack of repentance.
- Teach and explain contrite sorrow- a sadness of soul because one is broken over their sin against God.
- Teach and explain chastisement sorrow- a sadness of soul because one is experiencing the discipline of God leading to a product of righteousness in their living.

## Concept 18 – Understanding The Categories of Fears

- Teach and explain neutral fear- startle or fright; not considered wrong in the sight of God; not commanded in the sight of God.
- Teach and explain good fear- to fear God in the sense of reverence; to fear in the sense of concern, to fear in the sense of respect.

- Teach and explain wrong fear- to worry, to be intimidated by others.
- Teach and explain conscience fear- the fear of God's judgment as a result of a guilty conscience.

## Concept 19 – The Fear of Man

- Help people understand what it means to be afraid of man.
- Help people understand what it means to respect man as God.
- Help people understand what it means to depend on man as a source of life.
- Help people understand what it means to fear being exposed, rejected, physically hurt or oppressed, or being denied what we desire

## Concept 20 – The Six "R" S of Change

- Teach and explain what it means to realize – to be aware of the truth.
- Teach and explain what it means to remorse – to be convicted of the sin in connection with the truth
- Teach and explain what it means to renounce- to confess your sin accordingly
- Teach and explain what it means to repent- to turn away from sin.
- Teach and explain what it manes renew- to meditate on the truth that one is walk in to replace the sin
- Teach and explain what it means to replace- to put to practice the truth that overrides the sin

## Concept 21 – Forgiveness

- Teach the definition of forgiveness- to disregard, to let go, to release from, to pardon, to cancel a debt owed.
- Teach the person how to forgive.
- Teach the person the danger of not forgiving.
- Teach the person the difference between love and forgiveness.

## Concept 22 – How To Deal With the Past

- Help people identify what they did not want from the past that they still think about with revenge, anger, fear, or worry in the present and repent of it.
- Help people identify what they lost or did not receive in the past that they still treasuring in their hearts in a selfish self-centered ways in the present and repent of it.
- Help people identify past sinful actions and decisions that have caused present day problems and lead them to repent of it.
- Help people interpret their past and live in the present by the will of God.

### Concept 23 – The First and Greatest Commandment

- Teach various ways God loves us.
- Teach what it means to love God.

- Teach specific areas of life where one can love God.
- Help individuals learn how to put this to practice.

### Concept 24 – The Second and Great Commandment

- Teach the basic categories of Love.
- Teach the calling to Agape Love.

- Teach the characteristics of agape love.
- Help people understand how it applies to his life.

### Concept 25 – The Cycle of Relationships

- Explain the picture, preference, and presumption of a relationship.
- Explain the pain and practice of a relationship.

- Explain the position, priority, precepts of a relationship.
- Explain the peace and practice of a relationship.

### Concept 26 – The Four Kinds of Human Relationships

- Explain the principle of being open and unloving- right insight mean in presentation.
- Explain the principle of being closed and loving- have the desire to give truth and be beneficial to others but lacking time or ability to present it.

- Explain the principle of being open and loving- right insight kind in approach; providing what is beneficial to others accordingly.
- Explain the principle of being closed and unloving- having bitterness in heart towards others but acting is if one is okay with others.

### Concept 27 – The Categories of Conversations

- Explain the preference principle of conversation- conversations based on opinions.
- Explain the wisdom principle of conversation- conversations based on learning the best course of actions.

- Explain the conscience principle of conversation- conversations based on personal acquired standards.
- Explain the moral principle of conversation- conversations based on what is right and wrong according to Scripture.

### Concept 28 – Living By Purpose

- Teach and explain a Biblical View of God and His agenda.
- Help him lay out a mission plan for his life and family according to God's agenda.

- Help him identify the God-given roles and responsibilities for himself and family and write out a job descriptions of each according to Scripture.
- Help him organize his life around these particular roles and responsibilities in way that is God-honoring.

### Concept 29 – The Conscience

- Explain the definition of the conscience.
- Explain the categories the conscience uses to judge.

- Explain the why there is no such thing as false guilt.
- Help people apply this to their lives.

### Concept 30 – Self-Esteem, Self Image, and Self Love

- Teach and explain Self-Esteem – satisfaction or dissatisfaction with one's self according to one's choice to live right or wrong.
- Teach and explain Self-Image- understanding of who one's is or not; one's identify, and Self Love.
- Teach and explain Self Love- regard for one's self on a right and wrong level.
- Explain how they work together.

### Concept 31 – Conflict Resolution

- Teach the source of conflict- lustful desires
- Teach the steps it will take to identify the lustful desires that are creating the conflict.
- Layout the steps it will take to seek forgiveness from the parties involved within the conflict.
- Layout the plan to identify the associated problems and the solutions needed for problems.

### Concept 32 – Understanding and Dealing With Suffering

- Teach and explain the definition of suffering- to experience pain or distress as a result of choices within our control and choices beyond our control.
- Teach and explain why we suffer- sin, sanctification, or satan.
- Teach and explain how to think about suffering.
- Teach and explain how to deal with suffering.

### Concept 33 – Understanding and Dealing With Temptations

- Teach and explain the definition of temptation- an enticement presented to lead one into sin against God.
- Teach and explain about the lusts of our hearts.
- Teach and explain how lusts of our hearts are the very things that the devil uses against us by providing opportunities for us to satisfy those lusts.
- Teach and explain the signs and the solutions for temptation.

### Concept 34 – Why Do We Need Relationships?

- Teach and explain how people were created for God's glory
- Teach and explain that we need relationships to help us be productive for God.
- Teach and explain how we need relationships to help us when we fall into various troubles.
- Teach and explain how we need relationships to help us resist various temptations we face.

### Concept 35 – Biblical View of Friendship

- Teach and explain the definition of friendship- one who is intimately close to another in a productive God-honoring way
- Teach and explain how a good friend is first a friend of God.
- Teach and explain the various practices of a godly friend.
- Teach and explain the problems that can ruin a godly friendship.

### Concept 36 – Biblical View of Dating

- Teach and explain the 1Timothy 5:1 principle.
- Help singles learn how to be brothers and sisters and not lovers.
- Help singles move from friendship to engagement to marriage.
- Help them to not do anything on a date that they would have to stop doing if either of them were married to someone else.

## Concept 37 – Hypercriticism

- Define hypercriticism- being irritated and very critical of someone else who has the very same issues you have while denying that fact in your own life.
- Teach people how to identify hypercriticism.

- Help people work through the very issues they are criticizing in others.
- Help people serve others in their issues after they deal with those issues in their own life.

## Concept 38 – The Blessings of Disappointed Expectations

- Teach and explain why we have disappointments.
- Teach and explain how disappointments can reveal the sin issues of our hearts.

- Teach and explain how disappointments can lead us to deal with sin issues of our hearts.
- Help people learn to handle disappointments in a God-honoring way.

## Concept 39 – Learning To Be Content

- Define contentment- satisfaction within the soul apart from people and circumstances as a result of fellowship with God.
- Evaluate the Apostle Paul and identify his journey to contentment.

- Teach and explain the various Scriptures on contentment.
- Help people develop a track to move towards contentment.

## Concept 40 – Decision Making In the Will of God

- Teach people the sovereign will of God.
- Teach people the moral will of God.

- Teach people the non-moral will of God.
- Help people learn how to make decisions according to the concepts above.

## Concept 41 – Three Kinds of Fools

- Teach and explain the simple-minded fool.
- Teach and explain the scoffer.

- Teach and explain the ordinary fool.
- Help people identify where they stand.

## Concept 42 – Humility

- Teach the definition of humility – a mind set on Christ with submission and to the will of God.
- Give examples of humility.

- Help people learn where humility needs to take place.
- Help people learn how to walk in humility accordingly.

### Concept 43 – Prayer

- Teach people the prayer Jesus taught the disciples in Matthew 6:9-13.
- Teach people the principles about prayer found in Matthew 6:5-7.
- Teach people the importance of prayer.
- Give people a printed format to follow for prayer.

### Concept 44 – Trusting God

- Teach the principles of trust found in Proverbs 3:5-8.
- Teach people the areas in their life where they lack trust in God.
- Teach people the process of trusting God.
- Teach people various characteristics of God to trust according the situations of life they encounter.

### Concept 45 – Distinguishing Between Gossip and Sharing

- Teach and explain that Gossip is when negative or confidential information about people whether true or false is shared about them and no to them with intent to satisfy one's own selfish agenda.
- Teach and explain that Gossip is sharing negative or confidential information about people whether true or false with people who have no authority, involvement or solutions for resolution.
- Teach and explain It is not considered gossip when negative or confidential information that is proven to be true is shared with the proper leadership in order for that leadership to do what is right as prescribed by God in His Word to bring order, peace, reconciliation, church discipline or whatever is needed to the Glory of God, the good of the individual(s) involved and the good of the church.
- Teach and explain that it is okay to share your concern with a wise a person with the intent to learn how to change yourself or to do what is God-honoring; This must be done without vilifying, without accusing, or without complaining or condemning the person with whom there is a problem.

### Concept 46 – Hope

- Teach and explain the concept of hope based upon Romans 5:1-5.
- Teach and explain how the concept of putting hope in man's opinion will deceive us.
- Teach and explain how hope from God will draw us near to God.
- Teach and explain how hope from God will direct us to the return of Jesus Christ.

### Concept 47 – Spiritual Warfare

- Teach and explain the description of our enemy in spiritual warfare.
- Teach and explain the devises of our enemy in spiritual warfare.
- Teach and explain the desires of our hearts and the deceptions of the world in spiritual warfare.
- Teach and explain the directives for the battle and the defense the battle in spiritual warfare.

### Concept 48 – How To Establish and Build Trust in Relationships

- Teach and explain the definition of trust.
- Teach and explain the nature of trust in a relationship.
- Teach and explain where trust is not to be.
- Teach and explain the process of developing trust in a relationship as prescribed by God.

## Concept 49 – Embracing God

- Teach and explain the basic characteristics of God to embrace.
- Teach and explain the perspective to develop in embracing the characteristics of God.
- Teach and explain the practice you should have in embracing God.
- Teach and explain the patterns of relating with others that are the result of embracing God.

## Concept 50 – Categories of Sin

- Teach and explain imputed sin- classified as being in the position of sinner as a result of Adam.
- Teach and explain inherited sin- having a nature that is infested with sin as a result being born a sinner.
- Teach and explain individual sin –the actions of sin as a result imputed and inherited sin.
- Teach and explain the danger of sin- the impact it has on all aspects of life.

## Concept 51 – Categories of Peace

- Teach and explain peace with God- we are justified in Jesus Christ; God is no longer anger with us; we are reconciled to God forever.
- Teach and explain the peace of God- the tranquility of the soul as a result walking in obedience to the Spirit of God.
- Teach and explain peace with men- seeking to do what is right in the sight of God and others to keep or restore harmony within a relationship with others
- Teach and explain the peace of the conscience- tranquility of soul as result of submitting to the moral law of God
- Teach and explain the peace of world- tranquility of soul as result of the partaking of what the ungodly world's system has to offer.

## Concept 52 – The Four Stages of Spiritual Growth

- Teach and explain the teaching stage- One comes to the knowledge of truth in some aspect of life.
- Teach and explain the conviction stage- One comes to experience Godly sorrow in relation to the sin one has practiced instead of the truth one should have been living in some aspect of life.
- Teach and explain the correction stage- one puts off the sin in some aspect of life as result of learning the truth and being convicted of the sin in that particular area.
- Teach and explain the training stage- one puts to practice the truth in some aspect of life as a result of learning the truth and being convicted of sin in that particular area.

## Concept 53 – Guarding The Heart

- Teach and explain what it means to guard the heart.
- Teach and explain how one guards the heart.
- Teach and explain what one should purify and protect the heart from.
- Teach and explain what one should promote within and provide the heart.

## Concept 54 – Immaterial Pain, Material Pain, and Medication

- Teach and explain the nature of immaterial pain.
- Teach and explain the nature of material pain.
- Teach and explain the relationship between immaterial pain and material pain.
- Teach and explain the purpose of medication and the misuse of it with immaterial pain.

# THE DYNAMICS OF BIBLICAL COUNSELING

## Section Six

## Biblical Hope

**Definition of Hope**: *Expectation of a desired outcome*

**I. Hope that comes from God will not *disappoint* us (Romans 5:1-5).**
   A. This hope is ***provided*** by God's Grace to us (Romans 5:1-2).

   B. This hope is ***produced*** through tribulation, perseverance, and developed character (Romans 5:3-4).

   C. This hope is ***promoted*** by the Holy Spirit (Romans 5:5).

**II. Hope that comes from man's opinions will *deceive* us (Proverbs 16:25).**
   A. False hope is ***built*** on human ideas (Proverbs 14:12).
      1. All my problems would be solved if I had a better job.
      2. If I could have who and what I wanted in life, I would be happy.
      3. If my husband/wife would just give me my way, I would by happy and all my problems would be solved.

   B. False hope is ***based*** on an improper interpretation of scripture (2Peter 3:14-18).
      1. Since God owns it all, I should never be without.
      2. Since God is my Father, I should be healed of all diseases.
      3. God will give me anything I want if I just ask for it.
      4. We should call those things that are not as though they are.

   C. False hope is ***birthed*** by the passions of ungodly men (2 Peter 2:1-3).
      1. If I treat people right, I will not be mistreated by others.
      2. If I can believe it, then I can achieve it.
      3. There is a perfect mate for everyone.
      4. If I serve others, surely they will return the favor and serve me.

**III. Hope that comes from God will *draw* us near to God (Hebrews 7:11-19).**
   A. This hope ***drives*** us to depend on Christ (Hebrews 7:11-19).
      1. We can expect God to never leave us or forsake us (Hebrews 13:5-6).
      2. We can expect God to be our help in time of need (Hebrews 4:14-16).
      3. We can expect God to help us to make it through every trial and temptation we face (1Corinthians 10:13).
      4. We can expect God to provide all we need according to His riches in Glory in Christ Jesus (Philippians 4:19).

B. This hope *__develops__* stability in our faith (Hebrews 6:13-19).
   1. Because we have been saved we can expect to live in Heaven with Jesus (John 14:1-4).
   2. Because we have been saved we can expect to receive a glorified body like Jesus Christ (Philippians 3:20-21).
   3. Because we have been saved we can expect God to perfect the things concerning us (Psalm 138:8).

C. This hope *__deepens__* our confidence in Christ (Philippians 1:12-21).
   1. We can expect God to work all things together for our good (Romans 8:28).
   2. We can expect God to do exceedingly abundantly more than all we could ever ask or think (Ephesians 3:20).
   3. We can expect God to order our steps (Psalm 37:23).

**IV. Hope that comes from God will *direct* us to the return of Christ (1John 3:1-3).**
   A. This hope leads us to *__focus__* on Christ and His Glory (Titus 2:11-14).

   B. This hope leads us to *__favor__* the blessings we will receive at His return (1Peter 1:13).

   C. This hope leads us to *__forsake__* our sin so we can be like Christ (1John 3:1-3).

**V. You must take time to discern the kind of the Hope that lies within you?**

   A. **Examine** *your life and see what your hope is placed in*

   B. **Consider** *who or what you are depending on to bring it to pass*

   C. **Determine** *if what you are hoping for is promised to you by God*

# The Dynamics of Biblical Counseling

**Section Seven**

**A Policy for Biblical Discipleship Counseling**

**Are You Interested in Biblical Discipleship Counseling at _____ Church?**

Biblical counselors at _____ are available for a limited number of counseling cases. Our counselors (by design) are not certified by the State of _____; however, each counselor is trained and supervised by other counselors. Additionally, _____ counselors have had extensive training in biblical discipleship counseling and must meet various training requirements established by the Bible and the Director of the Ministry.

**Director of the Counseling Ministry**
Pastor _____, the director of the Ministry, teaches counseling at _____.
He received his _____ from_____.

**The Role of Scripture to the Counselor**
If you seek counseling from _____, we want you to know that all counseling will be conducted in accordance with the counselor's understanding of the Scriptures. All counseling will be biblically based, meaning that the Scriptures will be the authority in all cases. _____ Church does not subscribe to the teachings and methods of modern psychology or psychiatry, whether expressly secular or any attempted integration with biblical principles. Our counselors are not trained or licensed as psychotherapists or mental health professionals nor do they follow the methods of such persons. Also, our policy is to not make referrals to such persons.

If you (the counselee) are not sure that you will be interested in biblically-based counseling, counselee may first attend one or two sessions to discover what biblical discipleship counseling is like. If you or the counselor determines that you (the counselee) are unwilling to use the Bible as the final authority for your life, future counseling sessions will be terminated.

Additionally, each counseling session will conclude with the counselor assigning homework. If counselee is unwilling to complete the assigned homework, future counseling sessions will be terminated until the assigned homework has been completed to the satisfaction of the counselor. Any future sessions can be terminated by either party. However, if you (the counselee) are a member of _____ Church, the Pastor and/or Elders will be notified of the reasons for termination of your counseling sessions and all By-Laws and/or policies of _____ shall apply. If you are not a member of _____ Church, please note that written correspondence will be sent to your church notifying them of the termination of your counseling sessions and the reasons for said termination.

**Non-members of _____ Church**
Please note that _____ Church is committed to the spiritual health of its members thus, counseling of _____ Church members always takes precedence over all non-member related counseling services.

If counselee is a member in good standing with a church other than _____ Church, counselee is required to invite their Senior Pastor or an Elder to accompany them to the counseling sessions. **It is our first choice that your Senior Pastor/Elder from your local church or one of those in its leadership accompanies counselee to their counseling sessions.** However, if the Senior Pastor or an Elder is unavailable, the counselee must invite someone else in a leadership position from their local church.

We recognize and respect the authority and the discipline of counselee's church. If no one in a leadership position is available to attend counseling sessions with counselee, _____ Church's counselor, based solely on counselor's discernment of the matter, may decide to move forward with counselee. However, counselee must provide written permission from their Senior Pastor and/or Elder(s) to attend counseling at _____ Church. Counselee must submit to _____ Church a letter from their leadership (Pastor, Elders, or Deacons) stating that they are aware that counselee is receiving counseling from an outside source and that they approve of _____ Church counseling you – this letter must be signed and on the letterhead of counselee's church. In this letter counselee must also provide _____ Church with the name of a person in their church that will be their accountability partner and a phone number where _____ Church can contact this person. We do this because we firmly believe in the leadership of your church and we only want to come along side of them to offer assistance. Also, this will make transfer back to the pastoral care of counselee's church much easier to effect.

Additionally if counselee is unable to bring someone in leadership with them, or provide some form of accountability from their local congregation, _____ Church will not be able to facilitate the counseling process. This is due to the fact that _____ Church believes that the Senior Pastor/Elders are responsible for the spiritual well-being of their local congregation. Without the involvement or support of the Senior Pastor/Elders or someone in leadership from counselee's church, _____ Church would be assuming responsibility for counselee's spiritual well-being. _____ Church is not willing or biblically able to assume such a responsibility without the permission of counselee's church leadership.

**Non-member of a Church**
If counselee is currently not a member of a church or not a member in good standing with a church, _____ Church will expect counselee to attend their Church on a weekly basis while going through the counseling ministry. For example, if counselee is going to have 13 counseling sessions then _____ Church would expect that counselee would attend the church for 13 weeks. After such time _____ Church will be happy to assist counselee in finding a church home and of course, counselee is welcome to examine _____ Church as a possibility.

Our experience has been that for changes in people to be lasting, people need more than the help they receive in formal counseling. They need the total ministry of a church in which the preaching, teaching and fellowship are providing the same kind of help that is given in the counseling sessions. If counselee does not attend _____ Church on a regular basis (Sunday and Wednesday services at least three (3) times a month) all future counseling sessions will be terminated.

**Confidentiality**
Absolute confidentiality is not scriptural. In certain circumstances the Bible requires that facts be disclosed to select others (Matt. 18:15ff). In these areas we will follow the policy and procedures of _____ Church. When your church leadership inquires about the status of your sessions, we will disclose to them the information that is necessary for them to effectively and biblically fulfill their responsibility to shepherd you.

BY LAW, there are certain situations in which information about individuals undergoing counseling may be released with or without their permission. These situations are as follows: (Romans 13:1-3)

1. Where it is proven that children are physically abused, neglected, or sexually abused.

2. In emergency situations where there may be proven danger to the counselee or others, as with homicide or suicide, confidentiality may be broken.

3. If a court of law issues a legitimate subpoena relating to a child abuse case, we are required by law to provide the information specifically described in the subpoena.

4. If an unreported life-threatening felony has been committed, we are required by law to report it to the police.

At any time during the counseling, for reasons sufficient to himself/herself, the counselor – as also the counselee -- shall have the option of terminating counseling.

**Counseling Fees**
_____Church does not charge a specific fee for counseling. However, since there are costs involved in maintaining this ministry, counselees may want to express their thanks and help to maintain the ministry in a tangible way.

Donations should be made to _____ Church in matters such as these. Also, part of the weekly homework assignments may require counselee to purchase materials related to their counseling process. Counselees are expected to pay for these materials.

**Counselee Responsibility**
It should be understood that biblical discipleship counseling will involve giving scriptural teaching and making practical application of the same to each individual counselee. Counselee is held fully responsible for how he/she implements that counsel.

**Counselors in Training**
Here at _____ Church we not only provide biblical discipleship counseling, but are devoted to training biblical counselors. This means that the counselor may have one to two people assisting him/her in each counseling session.

**The Bible as the Authority in the Session**
We are confident that the Bible has all of the information necessary for life and godliness (2 Pet.1:3). There are no problems between persons or in persons that the Bible fails to address either in general or specific principles. Our counselors are not infallible, nor do they pretend to know all there is to know about biblical teaching and its applications to life, but they are well equipped and competent to help people change. They will make a point to differentiate between God's commands and their suggestions. Counselors will also honestly tell you if they are limited in their capacity to address a matter and will seek help from other trained counselors in matters where they feel it is needed.

**Medical/Legal Advice**
Please note that_____ Church does **not** give medical or legal advice.

If you are willing to enter into this kind of counseling, please fill out the forms attached below. Once you have filled out the forms please email the forms or mail them to us. (See our contact information.) Once you have emailed or mailed the forms, call us to see when/if scheduled times of counseling are available.

Thank you for your interest in the biblical discipleship counseling ministry of _____ Church.

**(Adapted from Wayne Mack at Wayne Mack Ministries)**

# Consent to Biblical Discipleship Counseling And Release of Liability Form

**What is Expected of You?**

It is our belief that change must begin with ourselves as we look to Jesus Christ for the power to change. Therefore, we ask you (counselee) to approach the counseling and encouragement process as an opportunity for personal change and spiritual growth. We ask that you refrain from the temptation of focusing on others, and instead we ask you to focus on what changes God desires to make in your life, in the midst of your circumstances. Be advised that you will be assigned "homework." Homework is a vital part of the change process; therefore, completion of the homework assignments before your next session is expected.

**CONFIDENTIALITY CLAUSE**

1) Absolute confidentiality is not scriptural. In certain circumstances the Bible requires that facts be disclosed to select others (Matthew 18:15ff). In these areas we follow the guidelines of _____ Church. When your church leadership inquires, we will disclose to them the information they need to effectively and biblically fulfill their responsibility to shepherd you.

2) The privacy and confidentiality of our conversations and records are a privilege of yours and are protected by our ethical principles in all but a few circumstances. BY LAW, there are certain situations in which information about individuals undergoing counseling may be released with or without their permission. These situations are as follows: (Romans 13:1-3)

- A. Where it is proven that children are physically abused, neglected, or sexually abused;
- B. In emergency situations where it is proven that there may be danger to the counselee or others, as with homicide or suicide, confidentiality may be broken;
- C. If a court of law issues a legitimate subpoena relating to a child abuse case, we are required by law to provide the information specifically described in the subpoena
- D. If an unreported life-threatening felony has been committed, we are required by law to report it to the police.

3) We reserve the right to consult with others or appropriate church ministry staff members regarding your sessions. This consultation will be held in the same level of confidence as your sessions. This will involve issues such as:

A. Church discipline matters
B. Seeking wise counsel to help address the matter in a thorough manner
C. Reporting to other leaders on the status of counseling when feasible and appropriate
D. Training of other counselors to learn how to handle cases of the same nature

**Resolution of Disagreements**

If a dispute should arise between the counselee and the counselor regarding the session or the counselor's advice or conduct, one should bring this dispute to the attention of the Director of the Biblical Discipleship Counseling Ministry of _____ Church. If the dispute cannot be resolved at this level, all parties agree to resolve such dispute by submitting to the Conflict Resolution Team of the Church_____ for full and final resolution and conciliation. Both, the counselee and the counselor agree not to take this matter to any secular court system. (1 Corinthians 6:1-7)

**Waiver of Liability**

The undersigned counselee, having sought biblical discipleship counseling as adhered to by _____ Church, a nonprofit religious organization, hereby acknowledges their understanding of the above stated conditions and therefore releases from liability the _____ Church and any/all participating churches, pastors, agents or employees, from a claim or litigation whatsoever arising from the undersigned's participation in the above-mentioned biblical discipleship counseling ministry.

It is further understood, in consideration for receiving any form of counseling from the _____ Church, the person (counselee) receiving the counseling agrees to release and waive any and all claims of any kind against the ministry, the staff, the pastoral/lay counselors or any participating church, which may arise from, result out of, or be related to conduct or advice/counsel given. Additionally, all counsel provided in by _____ Church is provided in accordance with the biblical principles adhered to by the Church and is not necessarily provided in adherence with any local or national psychological or psychiatric association.

That the undersigned agrees that he/she has read and thoroughly understands and agrees to what is expected of them, the confidentiality clause, the resolution of disagreements, _____ Church's policy for counseling that is placed on the website, and the contents of the waiver, and now willingly (without any coercion) consents to and requests said biblical discipleship counseling from _____ Church's biblical discipleship counseling ministry.

SIGNED on this _____ day of _____, AD, 20_____, at _____.
(County)_____

Signed Name_____

Printed Name_____

Before me, the undersigned authority on this day personally appeared _____, known to me to be the person whose name is subscribed to the foregoing instrument of writing and acknowledged to me that he executed the same for the purposes and consideration thereon expressed. SWORN TO AND SUBSCRIBED BEFORE ME, under my official hand and seal of office this the _____ day of _____, 20_____.

_____
NOTARY PUBLIC In and for the STATE OF _____

Printed Name: _____

My Commission expires: _____

## PERSONAL DATA INVENTORY
Please complete this inventory carefully

**PERSONAL IDENTIFICATION:**

Name _____ Birth Date _____

Address _____ Zip _____

Age _____ Sex _____ Referred By _____

Marital Status:

Single ____ Engaged ____ Married ____ Separated ____ Divorced ____ Widowed ____

Education: (last year completed): _____

Home Phone _____ Business Phone _____

Employer _____ Position _____ Years ____

In case of emergency, please contact: _____(name)

_____(Phone numbers)

**MARRIAGE AND FAMILY:**

Spouse _____ Birth Date _____

Age _____ Occupation _____ How long employed _____

Home Phone _____ Business Phone _____

Date of Marriage _____ Length of dating _____

Give brief statement of circumstances of meeting and dating _____

_____

Have either of you been previously married _____ To Whom _____

Have you ever been separated _____ Filed for divorce _____

Information about children:

Name                     Age    Sex    Living    Yrs. Ed.    Step-child

_____

_____

_____

_____

Describe relationship to your father _____
_____

Describe relationship to your mother _____
_____

Number of siblings _____ Your sibling order _____
Did you live with anyone other than parents _____
_____

Are your parents living _____ Do they live locally _____

## HEALTH

Describe your health _____
Do you have any chronic conditions _____ what _____
List important illnesses and injuries or handicaps _____
_____

Date last medical exam _____ Report _____
Physician's name and address _____
Current medication(s) and dosage _____
_____

Have you ever used drugs for other than medical purposes _____
If yes, please explain _____
_____

Have you ever been arrested _____
Do you drink alcoholic beverages _____ If so, how frequently and how much _____
_____

Do you drink coffee _____ How much _____
Other caffeine drinks _____ How much _____
Do you smoke _____ What _____ Frequency _____
Have you ever had interpersonal problems on the job _____
_____

Have you ever had a severe emotional upset _____ If yes, explain _____
_____

Have you ever seen a psychiatrist or counselor _____ If yes, explain _____
_____

Are you willing to sign a release of information form so that your counselor may write for social, psychiatric, or other medical records _____

## SPIRITUAL:

Denominational preference _____

Church attending _____

Church attendance per month (circle one)    0   1   2   3   4   5   6   7   8+

Do you believe in God _____ Do you pray _____

Would you say you are a Christian or still in the process of becoming a Christian _____
_____

Have you been baptized _____

How often do you read the Bible _____ never _____ Occasionally _____ Daily

Explain any recent changes in your religious life _____
_____

## WOMEN ONLY:

Have you had any menstrual difficulties _____ Do you experience tension, tendency to cry, other symptoms prior to your cycle, please explain _____

Is your husband willing to come for counseling _____

Is he in favor of your coming _____ If no, explain _____
_____

**Problem Checklist**

| | |
|---|---|
| ____ Anger | ____ Guilt |
| ____ Anxiety | ____ Health |
| ____ Apathy | ____ Homosexuality |
| ____ Appetite | ____ Impotence |
| ____ Bitterness | ____ In-laws |
| ____ Change in lifestyle | ____ Loneliness |
| ____ Children | ____ Lust |
| ____ Communication | ____ Memory |
| ____ Conflict (fights) | ____ Moodiness |
| ____ Deception | ____ Perfectionism |
| ____ Decision-making | ____ Rebellion |
| ____ Depression | ____ Sex |
| ____ Drunkenness | ____ Sleep |
| ____ Envy | ____ Wife Abuse |
| ____ Fear | ____ A vice |
| ____ Finances | ____ Other |
| ____ Gluttony | |

**BRIEFLY ANSWER THE FOLLOWING QUESTIONS:**

1. What is the problem or concern that brings you here today?

_____

_____

_____

_____

2. What have you done about this problem?

_____
_____
_____
_____

3. What are your expectations from counseling?

_____
_____
_____
_____

4. Is there any other information we should know about?

_____
_____
_____

**SPIRITUAL CONVICTIONS QUESTIONNAIRE:** (Please use the back of this sheet if necessary.)

1. Describe Who God is:

_____
_____

2. Describe Who Jesus Christ is:

_____
_____

3. Describe the kind of relationship you have with God and His Son Jesus Christ:

_____
_____

4. What is the Definition of a Christian?

_____

_____

5. I am or (I am not) a Christian because:

_____

_____

6. What do you believe about the Bible?

_____

_____

7. What is your definition of sin?

_____

_____

8. What sins do you struggle with the most?

_____

_____

9. How do you handle sin in your life?

_____

_____

10. How do you handle guilt?

_____

_____

11. What do you tend to pray about the most?

_____

_____

12. What do you seek to accomplish in life?

_____

_____

13. I do attend or I do not attend church because:

_____
_____
_____


14. I allow Christians or I do not allow Christians to be involved in my life because:_____

_____

15. The changes I would like to make in my life are:_____

_____
_____


What have you learned about yourself and what have you learned about your partner? What changes do you need to make in light of this study?

_____
_____
_____
_____
_____
_____
_____
_____
_____

**(Adapted from Wayne Mack & Jay Adams)**

# A Case Report form

## *Biblical Counseling Case Form*
(Adapted from ACBC form)

Counselor's Name _____
Name of Counselee_____
Date of Appt. _____   Session # _____
Time of Appt. _____

1. Significant background information

2. Summary of reason they came for counseling (presentation problem)

3. What main problem(s) were discussed in this session?

4. What can they control in this situation?

5. What are they not able control in this situation?

6. What are their neutral, unloving, loving responses in this situation?

7. What are the consequences of their choices in this situation?

8. What unbiblical habits of are you seeing in the counselee (pre-conditioning)?

    a. Thoughts, motives and desires?
    b. Communication?
    c. Behavior/manor of life?
    d. Relationship patterns?
    e. Service of others?

9. What idolatrous-lust is emerging? (I must have _____ (Lust), If _____ (Idol) does not provide _____ (Lust) I will be upset!)

10. What key concepts/worksheet did you use when discussing the specific problems?(Tied to #4)

11. What stage of spiritual growth are they in according to the problem discussed? What stage of spiritual growth are you to lead them to as a result? (Teaching stage, conviction stage, correction stage, training stage).

12. What homework was given and how did it specifically apply to the problems and the stage of spiritual growth the person is in and is to be lead into (hope homework, doctrinal homework, awareness homework, embracing God homework, action oriented homework, relation oriented homework)?

13. What specifics acts of love towards God and others will you eventually be leading them to/or are leading them to walk in?

14. How does forgiveness play out in this if at all?

15. If someone asked the counselee right after the session, "What did you learn that you needed to change?" what would you want him to say?

16. How was hope or encouragement given in this session?

17. How is the overall counseling process progressing and what issues have been sufficiently addressed by you and changed by the counselee in the areas of thoughts, motives, desires, communication, behavior, lifestyle, relationship patterns, or serving?

18. What are your goals for future sessions?

If the session is not moving, review Jay Adam's "50 Failure Factors" at the back of the Christian Counseling Manual.

# THE DYNAMICS OF BIBLICAL COUNSELING

## Section Eight

## Scenario 1

Kenneth is a 45 year old male. Yesterday he was told by his boss that the company would be downsizing and would no longer be needing his services. Kenneth was not shaken he politely asked when his last day would be and kindly walked out of the office. Over the last few weeks Kenneth has been experiencing many panic attacks on his way to work. His friends report that Kenneth has been eating more than usual, oversleeping and coming in late to work. Kenneth told his friends that the boss has put a camera in Kenneth's house and is watching his every move. Kenneth also believes that his boss has hired hit men to come after him. Kenneth is scared to go outside because he believes his boss is following him. He has been calling in sick and finding reasons why he cannot leave his home. Kenneth has gained about ten pounds in the last five weeks and is refusing to take a bath or clean himself up. Kenneth tries to find every excuse possible not to communicate with his boss.

**Step 1: _Connect_ with the Counselee(s): Identify 5 questions you can ask to get to know the counselee(s)**

    Question 1:

    Question 2:

    Question 3:

    Question 4:

    Question 5:

**Step 2: _Console_ the Counselee(s): Think through some words of encouragement you can provide within the session:**

**Step 3:** *Collect* **data from the Counselee(s) in regards to their problems and concerns. Identify ten questions you can ask to get to the root of the problem(s) and concern(s):**

Question 1:

Question 2:

Question 3:

Question 4:

Question 5:

Question 6:

Question 7:

Question 8:

Question 9:

Question 10:

**Step 4:** *Categorize* **data from the Counselee into Biblical terms and perspectives as you are thinking through Biblical solutions.**

    a. As you look at the characteristics of the situation/problem are there any expressions of uncaused fleeing being demonstrated? If so, write them down.

    b. As you look at the characteristics of the situation/problem are there any expressions of uncaused fear being demonstrated? If so, write them down.

    c. As you look at the characteristics of the situation/problem are there any expressions of a sense of guilt being demonstrated? If so, write them down.

    d. As you look at the characteristics of the situation/problem are there any secondary unloving/sinful attitudes, words, actions (unloving /sinful attitudes, words or actions being expressed as a result of the main unloving/sinful attitude, word, or action) being demonstrated? If so, write them down.

**Step 5: <u>Communicate</u> to counselee(s) what the Bible defines as the source and the symptoms of the problems in Biblical terms and *clarify* what the Biblical solutions are to those problems.**

    a. What is the root of the problem (First Level Sin)?

    b. What are the byproducts (guilt, au fear, au fleeing, physiological matters, secondary sins ect.) that are occurring as a result the problem?

    c. Identify at least Ten Scriptures that can communicate the problem and clarify what the Biblical solutions are for this particular problem.

    d. Identify the key biblical concepts you need to teach in this session to communicate the problem and to clarify the solution.

        Concept 1:

        Concept 2:

        Concept 3:

        Concept 4:

Step 6: *__Challenge__* the Counselee to a commitment to confess, repent, and replace sin with love for God and others. Think through some words of challenge for this particular session:

Step 7: __Construct__ homework for the counselee(s) to apply to their lives that will lead them into confession, repentance, and replacement of sin with love for God and others: Identify what will fit for this closing session:

    a. *__Hope Homework__* –

    b. *__Doctrinal Homework__* –

    c. *__Awareness Homework__* –

    d. *__Embracing God Homework__* –

    e. *__Action Oriented Homework__* –

    f. *__Relational Orientated Homework__* –

**Step 8: *Conjoin* the counselee(s) to the Body of Christ accordingly. According to this session choose what best fits for the counselee(s)**

    a. *Membership* – the counselee would be lead to join a local church that they may experience love and enjoy the blessings of God-honoring relationships.

    b. *Maturity* – the counselee would be lead to get involved in discipleship courses in a local church that would lead them into loving God, loving others on a consistent basis and living a life that reflects the character of Christ.

    c. *Magnification* – the counselee would be led to come to appreciate, value, and adore the character of God through heart-felt genuine worship of Him in a local church.

    d. *Ministry* – the counselee would be led to join a ministry where they can develop in bearing burdens and meeting needs according to the various relationships they will develop through the local church.

    e. *Missions* – the counselee would be led into supporting a local church in sharing and defending the Christian Faith

# The Dynamics of Biblical Counseling

## Section Nine

## Scenario 2

Phil and Erica have been married for 10 years. They met in college where they instantly became good friends. After two years of friendship they decided to get married. Their marriage has had it challenges but the relationship is stable. Over the last few weeks Phil has been avoiding communication with Erica. He simply does not want to talk. He has been coming home later than usual around the time Erica is going to bed or has fallen asleep. Phil has mentioned to his friends that when he is on his way home he experiences panic attacks. So instead of going home he finds himself stopping at the local strip club before he gets home. Lately when he talks to his wife he gets this overwhelming compulsion to clean the house from top to bottom and to take several baths within hour of their conversation. His wife does not understand what is happening with Phil. She mentioned that this all started around the time Erica acknowledged that she was pregnant.

**Step 1:** *Connect* **with the Counselee(s): Identify 5 questions you can ask to get to know the counselee(s)**

Question 1:

Question 2:

Question 3:

Question 4:

Question 5:

**Step 2:** *Console* **the Counselee(s): Think through some words of encouragement you can provide within the session:**

**Step 3:** *Collect* **data from the Counselee(s) in regards to their problems and concerns. Identify ten questions you can ask to get to the root of the problem(s) and concern(s):**

Question 1:

Question 2:

Question 3:

Question 4:

Question 5:

Question 6:

Question 7:

Question 8:

Question 9:

Question 10:

**Step 4: _Categorize_ data from the Counselee into Biblical terms and perspectives as you are thinking through Biblical solutions.**

    a. As you look at the characteristics of the situation/problem are there any expressions of uncaused fleeing being demonstrated? If so, write them down.

    b. As you look at the characteristics of the situation/problem are there any expressions of uncaused fear being demonstrated? If so, write them down.

c. As you look at the characteristics of the situation/problem are there any expressions of a sense of guilt being demonstrated? If so, write them down.

d. As you look at the characteristics of the situation/problem are there any secondary unloving/sinful attitudes, words, actions (unloving /sinful attitudes, words or actions being expressed as a result of the main unloving/sinful attitude, word, or action) being demonstrated? If so, write them down.

**Step 5: Communicate to counselee(s) what the Bible defines as the source and the symptoms of the problems in Biblical terms and *clarify* what the Biblical solutions are to those problems.**

a. What is the root of the problem (First Level Sin)?

b. What are the byproducts (guilt, au fear, au fleeing, physiological matters, secondary sins ect.) that are occurring as a result the problem?

c. Identify at least Ten Scriptures that can communicate the problem and clarify what the Biblical solutions are for this particular problem.

d. Identify the key biblical concepts you need to teach in this session to communicate the problem and to clarify the solution.

   Concept 1:

   Concept 2:

   Concept 3:

   Concept 4:

**Step 6:** <u>*Challenge*</u> **the Counselee to a commitment to confess, repent, and replace sin with love for God and others. Think through some words of challenge for this particular session:**

**Step 7:** <u>Construct</u> **homework for the counselee(s) to apply to their lives that will lead them into confession, repentance, and replacement of sin with love for God and others: Identify what will fit for this closing session:**

   a. <u>*Hope Homework*</u> –

   b. <u>*Doctrinal Homework*</u> –

   c. <u>*Awareness Homework*</u> –

75

d. *<u>Embracing God Homework</u>* –

e. *<u>Action Oriented Homework</u>* –

f. *<u>Relational Orientated Homework</u>* –

**Step 8: *<u>Conjoin</u>* the counselee(s) to the Body of Christ accordingly. According to this session choose what best fits for the counselee(s)**

a. *<u>Membership</u>* – the counselee would be lead to join a local church that they may experience love and enjoy the blessings of God-honoring relationships.

b. *<u>Maturity</u>* – the counselee would be lead to get involved in discipleship courses in a local church that would lead them into loving God, loving others on a consistent basis and living a life that reflects the character of Christ.

c. *<u>Magnification</u>* – the counselee would be led to come to appreciate, value, and adore the character of God through heart-felt genuine worship of Him in a local church.

d. *<u>Ministry</u>* – the counselee would be led to join a ministry where they can develop in bearing burdens and meeting needs according to the various relationships they will develop through the local church.

e. *<u>Missions</u>* – the counselee would be led into supporting a local church in sharing and defending the Christian Faith.

# THE DYNAMICS OF BIBLICAL COUNSELING

## Section Ten

### Scenario 3

Brad is ten years old. His mother and father are both loving and supporting parents. His mother is a housewife and his dad works with a major engineering firm. Over the last few months Brad's parent have been called to speak with his teacher and the principle more than 4 times. The teacher mentioned that Brad does not pay close attention to the instructions given by the teacher. He keeps losing his pencils and worksheets when it is time to do his work. She mentioned that Brad can't seem to sit still in his chair. He tends to wander off to talk to others students when it is time to do his work. Brad tends interrupt the teacher and other students when they are trying to discuss the assignments to work on. The teacher also mentioned that he has not turned in any of his homework assignments over the last three days. Yet when Brad is playing video games or watching TV he does not display any of these behaviors.

**Step 1:** *<u>Connect</u>* **with the Counselee(s): Identify 5 questions you can ask to get to know the counselee(s)**

    Question 1:

    Question 2:

    Question 3:

    Question 4:

    Question 5:

**Step 2:** *<u>Console</u>* **the Counselee(s): Think through some words of encouragement you can provide within the session:**

**Step 3:** *Collect* **data from the Counselee(s) in regards to their problems and concerns. Identify ten questions you can ask to get to the root of the problem(s) and concern(s):**

Question 1:

Question 2:

Question 3:

Question 4:

Question 5:

Question 6:

Question 7:

Question 8:

Question 9:

Question 10:

**Step 4: *Categorize* data from the Counselee into Biblical terms and perspectives as you are thinking through Biblical solutions.**

    a. As you look at the characteristics of the situation/problem are there any expressions of uncaused fleeing being demonstrated? If so, write them down.

    b. As you look at the characteristics of the situation/problem are there any expressions of uncaused fear being demonstrated? If so, write them down.

    c. As you look at the characteristics of the situation/problem are there any expressions of a sense of guilt being demonstrated? If so, write them down.

    d. As you look at the characteristics of the situation/problem are there any secondary unloving/sinful attitudes, words, actions (unloving /sinful attitudes, words or actions being expressed as a result of the main unloving/sinful attitude, word, or action) being demonstrated? If so, write them down.

**Step 5: *Communicate* to counselee(s) what the Bible defines as the source and the symptoms of the problems in Biblical terms and *clarify* what the Biblical solutions are to those problems.**

    a. What is the root of the problem (First Level Sin)?

    b. What are the byproducts (guilt, au fear, au fleeing, physiological matters, secondary sins ect.) that are occurring as a result the problem?

c.  Identify at least Ten Scriptures that can communicate the problem and clarify what the Biblical solutions are for this particular problem.

d.  Identify the key biblical concepts you need to teach in this session to communicate the problem and to clarify the solution.

   Concept 1:

   Concept 2:

   Concept 3:

   Concept 4:

**Step 6: _Challenge_ the Counselee to a commitment to confess, repent, and replace sin with love for God and others. Think through some words of challenge for this particular session:**

Step 7: **Construct** homework for the counselee(s) to apply to their lives that will lead them into confession, repentance, and replacement of sin with love for God and others: Identify what will fit for this closing session:

   a. *Hope Homework* –

   b. *Doctrinal Homework* –

   c. *Awareness Homework* –

   d. *Embracing God Homework* –

   e. *Action Oriented Homework* –

   f. *Relational Orientated Homework* –

**Step 8: *Conjoin* the counselee(s) to the Body of Christ accordingly. According to this session choose what best fits for the counselee(s)**

    a. *Membership* – the counselee would be lead to join a local church that they may experience love and enjoy the blessings of God-honoring relationships.

    b. *Maturity* – the counselee would be lead to get involved in discipleship courses in a local church that would lead them into loving God, loving others on a consistent basis and living a life that reflects the character of Christ.

    c. *Magnification* – the counselee would be led to come to appreciate, value, and adore the character of God through heart-felt genuine worship of Him in a local church.

    d. *Ministry* – the counselee would be led to join a ministry where they can develop in bearing burdens and meeting needs according to the various relationships they will develop through the local church.

    e. *Missions* – the counselee would be led into supporting a local church in sharing and defending the Christian Faith

# The Dynamics of Biblical Counseling

## Section Eleven

## Scenario 4

Emmit is 40 years old. He is married to Betty who is 39 years old. She has a daughter that is 19 years old from a previous marriage. She comes to visit from time to time. She lives with her biological father. Emmit has been having a hard time relating properly with his wife. Over the last couple of days things have been very tense between them. Emmit withdraws and goes to read a book or work on other things. He changes the subject when asks certain questions. He is constantly fighting with her and complains of her lack of respect for him and his decisions. He frequently leaves the house and returns very late. He even has a drink or two before he comes home. Emmit complains that when her 19 year old daughter visits his wife tends to disrespect him and favor her. Whenever the daughter is around there is confusion and disorder. His wife blames him for their daughter not staying with them and he challenges her. This behavior has been happening since the daughter has asked to come and live with them.

**Step 1: _Connect_ with the Counselee(s): Identify 5 questions you can ask to get to know the counselee(s)**

Question 1:

Question 2:

Question 3:

Question 4:

Question 5:

**Step 2: _Console_ the Counselee(s): Think through some words of encouragement you can provide within the session:**

**Step 3:** <u>*Collect*</u> **data from the Counselee(s) in regards to their problems and concerns. Identify ten questions you can ask to get to the root of the problem(s) and concern(s):**

Question 1:

Question 2:

Question 3:

Question 4:

Question 5:

Question 6:

Question 7:

Question 8:

Question 9:

Question 10:

**Step 4:** *Categorize* **data from the Counselee into Biblical terms and perspectives as you are thinking through Biblical solutions.**

    a. As you look at the characteristics of the situation/problem are there any expressions of uncaused fleeing being demonstrated? If so, write them down.

    b. As you look at the characteristics of the situation/problem are there any expressions of uncaused fear being demonstrated? If so, write them down.

    c. As you look at the characteristics of the situation/problem are there any expressions of a sense of guilt being demonstrated? If so, write them down.

    d. As you look at the characteristics of the situation/problem are there any secondary unloving/sinful attitudes, words, actions (unloving /sinful attitudes, words or actions being expressed as a result of the main unloving/sinful attitude, word, or action) being demonstrated? If so, write them down.

**Step 5: Communicate to counselee(s) what the Bible defines as the source and the symptoms of the problems in Biblical terms and *clarify* what the Biblical solutions are to those problems.**

    a.   What is the root of the problem (First Level Sin)?

    b.   What are the byproducts (guilt, au fear, au fleeing, physiological matters, and secondary sins etc.) that are occurring as a result the problem?

    c.   Identify at least Ten Scriptures that can communicate the problem and clarify what the Biblical solutions are for this particular problem.

    d.   Identify the key biblical concepts you need to teach in this session to communicate the problem and to clarify the solution.

        Concept 1:

        Concept 2:

        Concept 3:

        Concept 4:

Step 6: <u>*Challenge*</u> the Counselee to a commitment to confess, repent, and replace sin with love for God and others. Think through some words of challenge for this particular session:

Step 7: <u>Construct</u> homework for the counselee(s) to apply to their lives that will lead them into confession, repentance, and replacement of sin with love for God and others: Identify what will fit for this closing session:

  a. *<u>Hope Homework</u>* –

  b. *<u>Doctrinal Homework</u>* –

  c. *<u>Awareness Homework</u>* –

  d. *<u>Embracing God Homework</u>* –

  e. *<u>Action Oriented Homework</u>* –

  f. *<u>Relational Orientated Homework</u>* –

**Step 8: _Conjoin_ the counselee(s) to the Body of Christ accordingly. According to this session choose what best fits for the counselee(s)**

    a. _Membership_ – the counselee would be lead to join a local church that they may experience love and enjoy the blessings of God-honoring relationships.

    b. _Maturity_ – the counselee would be lead to get involved in discipleship courses in a local church that would lead them into loving God, loving others on a consistent basis and living a life that reflects the character of Christ.

    c. _Magnification_ – the counselee would be led to come to appreciate, value, and adore the character of God through heart-felt genuine worship of Him in a local church.

    d. _Ministry_ – the counselee would be led to join a ministry where they can develop in bearing burdens and meeting needs according to the various relationships they will develop through the local church.

    e. _Missions_ – the counselee would be led into supporting a local church in sharing and defending the Christian Faith

# THE DYNAMICS OF BIBLICAL COUNSELING

## Section Twelve

## Scenario 5

Barry has been working on his job for the last 15 years. He has a really good record and is even been considered for a major promotion. Over the last month on his way to work Barry experiences restlessness and muscle tension. When his boss ask him job related questions he has difficulty concentrating and finds his mind going blank. His coworkers notice that he gets real irritable when it is time to go into staff meetings. Barry has a hard time falling asleep at night and is very tired in the morning. When Barry comes home he seems to relax but when it is time for work finds himself fantasizing about dying. Over the last month Barry has been having difficulty with a co-worker that his boss asked him to train.

**Step 1:** *Connect* **with the Counselee(s): Identify 5 questions you can ask to get to know the counselee(s)**

    Question 1:

    Question 2:

    Question 3:

    Question 4:

    Question 5:

**Step 2:** *Console* **the Counselee(s): Think through some words of encouragement you can provide within the session:**

**Step 3:** *Collect* **data from the Counselee(s) in regards to their problems and concerns. Identify ten questions you can ask to get to the root of the problem(s) and concern(s):**

Question 1:

Question 2:

Question 3:

Question 4:

Question 5:

Question 6:

Question 7:

Question 8:

Question 9:

Question 10:

**Step 4:** *Categorize* data from the Counselee into Biblical terms and perspectives as you are thinking through Biblical solutions.

    a. As you look at the characteristics of the situation/problem are there any expressions of uncaused fleeing being demonstrated? If so, write them down.

    b. As you look at the characteristics of the situation/problem are there any expressions of uncaused fear being demonstrated? If so, write them down.

    c. As you look at the characteristics of the situation/problem are there any expressions of a sense of guilt being demonstrated? If so, write them down.

    d. As you look at the characteristics of the situation/problem are there any secondary unloving/sinful attitudes, words, actions (unloving /sinful attitudes, words or actions being expressed as a result of the main unloving/sinful attitude, word, or action) being demonstrated? If so, write them down.

**Step 5: <u>Communicate</u> to counselee(s) what the Bible defines as the source and the symptoms of the problems in Biblical terms and *clarify* what the Biblical solutions are to those problems.**

    a. What is the root of the problem (First Level Sin)?

    b. What are the byproducts (guilt, au fear, au fleeing, physiological matters, and secondary sins etc.) that are occurring as a result the problem?

    c. Identify at least Ten Scriptures that can communicate the problem and clarify what the Biblical solutions are for this particular problem.

    d. Identify the key biblical concepts you need to teach in this session to communicate the problem and to clarify the solution.

        Concept 1:

        Concept 2:

        Concept 3:

        Concept 4:

**Step 6:** <u>*Challenge*</u> the Counselee to a commitment to confess, repent, and replace sin with love for God and others. Think through some words of challenge for this particular session:




**Step 7:** <u>Construct</u> homework for the counselee(s) to apply to their lives that will lead them into confession, repentance, and replacement of sin with love for God and others: Identify what will fit for this closing session:

a. <u>*Hope Homework*</u> –


b. <u>*Doctrinal Homework*</u> –


c. <u>*Awareness Homework*</u> –


d. <u>*Embracing God Homework*</u> –


e. <u>*Action Oriented Homework*</u> –


f. <u>*Relational Orientated Homework*</u> –

**Step 8: _Conjoin_ the counselee(s) to the Body of Christ accordingly. According to this session choose what best fits for the counselee(s)**

    a. _Membership_ – the counselee would be lead to join a local church that they may experience love and enjoy the blessings of God-honoring relationships.

    b. _Maturity_ – the counselee would be lead to get involved in discipleship courses in a local church that would lead them into loving God, loving others on a consistent basis and living a life that reflects the character of Christ.

    c. _Magnification_ – the counselee would be led to come to appreciate, value, and adore the character of God through heart-felt genuine worship of Him in a local church.

    d. _Ministry_ – the counselee would be led to join a ministry where they can develop in bearing burdens and meeting needs according to the various relationships they will develop through the local church.

    e. _Missions_ – the counselee would be led into supporting a local church in sharing and defending the Christian Faith

# The Dynamics of Biblical Counseling

## Section Thirteen

## Scenario 6

Barbara has been living in an apartment with no social connection with family or friends for about 4 years. She does not talk to her family for more than 10 minutes a week. When she is in a social setting she sits in the corner and watches other people she does not interact with. She is the first to come and the first to leave a social gathering. If anyone tries to talk to her that she does not know she starts to stutter and then shuts down. Barbara does not talk much to people on her job. When people try to connect with her on the job she politely smiles and gives shorts answers. She then figures out a way to get out of the conversation. When she stays away from her house for more than 24 hours she begins to have panic attacks, heart palpitations and even colds sweats. Barbara has been that way since she was raped over 4 years ago.

**Step 1: _Connect_ with the Counselee(s): Identify 5 questions you can ask to get to know the counselee(s)**

    Question 1:

    Question 2:

    Question 3:

    Question 4:

    Question 5:

**Step 2: _Console_ the Counselee(s): Think through some words of encouragement you can provide within the session:**

**Step 3:** *Collect* **data from the Counselee(s) in regards to their problems and concerns. Identify ten questions you can ask to get to the root of the problem(s) and concern(s):**

Question 1:

Question 2:

Question 3:

Question 4:

Question 5:

Question 6:

Question 7:

Question 8:

Question 9:

Question 10:

**Step 4: *Categorize* data from the Counselee into Biblical terms and perspectives as you are thinking through Biblical solutions.**

    a. As you look at the characteristics of the situation/problem are there any expressions of uncaused fleeing being demonstrated? If so, write them down.

    b. As you look at the characteristics of the situation/problem are there any expressions of uncaused fear being demonstrated? If so, write them down.

    c. As you look at the characteristics of the situation/problem are there any expressions of a sense of guilt being demonstrated? If so, write them down.

    d. As you look at the characteristics of the situation/problem are there any secondary unloving/sinful attitudes, words, actions (unloving /sinful attitudes, words or actions being expressed as a result of the main unloving/sinful attitude, word, or action) being demonstrated? If so, write them down.

**Step 5: Communicate to counselee(s) what the Bible defines as the source and the symptoms of the problems in Biblical terms and *clarify* what the Biblical solutions are to those problems.**

    a. What is the root of the problem (First Level Sin)?

    b. What are the byproducts (guilt, au fear, au fleeing, physiological matters, and secondary sins etc.) that are occurring as a result the problem?

    c. Identify at least Ten Scriptures that can communicate the problem and clarify what the Biblical solutions are for this particular problem.

    d. Identify the key biblical concepts you need to teach in this session to communicate the problem and to clarify the solution.

        Concept 1:

        Concept 2:

        Concept 3:

        Concept 4:

Step 6: _Challenge_ the Counselee to a commitment to confess, repent, and replace sin with love for God and others. Think through some words of challenge for this particular session:




Step 7: _Construct_ homework for the counselee(s) to apply to their lives that will lead them into confession, repentance, and replacement of sin with love for God and others: Identify what will fit for this closing session:

    a. _Hope Homework_ –


    b. _Doctrinal Homework_ –


    c. _Awareness Homework_ –


    d. _Embracing God Homework_ –


    e. _Action Oriented Homework_ –


    f. _Relational Orientated Homework_ –

**Step 8: *Conjoin* the counselee(s) to the Body of Christ accordingly. According to this session choose what best fits for the counselee(s)**

    a. *Membership* – the counselee would be lead to join a local church that they may experience love and enjoy the blessings of God-honoring relationships.

    b. *Maturity* – the counselee would be lead to get involved in discipleship courses in a local church that would lead them into loving God, loving others on a consistent basis and living a life that reflects the character of Christ.

    c. *Magnification* – the counselee would be led to come to appreciate, value, and adore the character of God through heart-felt genuine worship of Him in a local church.

    d. *Ministry* – the counselee would be led to join a ministry where they can develop in bearing burdens and meeting needs according to the various relationships they will develop through the local church.

    e. *Missions* – the counselee would be led into supporting a local church in sharing and defending the Christian Faith

# THE DYNAMICS OF BIBLICAL COUNSELING

## Section Fourteen

## What Is The Biblical Framework?

It is a picture of what happens in the immaterial heart of man as a result of his choice to obey or to disobey God. The Biblical Framework shows how the conscience produces in a person's immaterial heart a sense of guilt, apparently uncaused fear, and a desire to flee from the apparently uncaused fear and a sense of guilt when he is walking in disobedience to God. The Biblical Framework shows how the conscience produces in a person's immaterial heart a sense of peace, a confidence before God and a desire to draw near to God when he is walking in obedience to God through the power of the Holy Spirit. The Biblical Framework reveals that all sin is basically demonstrating a lack love for God and others. Since the Bible commands us to love God and love others (which are the two greatest commandments) any sin we commit is a direct violation of these two commandments which in essence is a lack of love for God and others. Therefore, proper response of obedience to God's commands demonstrates a love for God and a love for others. Listen to this quote from Rich Thomson:

> The Biblical Framework is a diagram of the inner workings of the human heart (man's immaterial being). It pictures how man's conscience, in response to the loving and unloving choices he makes, instinctively and instantaneously produces in his heart a knowledge and sense of peace or of guilt, confidence before God or a fear of His judgment (apparently uncaused fear), and a desire to draw near to Him or to flee from that sense of guilt and fear of His judgment (apparently uncaused fleeing). These conscience-stimulated inner reactions, then, drive many of man's deepest thoughts, motivations, desires, and emotions – both those that are loving, open, and beneficial and those that are unloving, detrimental, and/or hidden in unexplained fears (or anxieties), obscure choices, and irrational behaviors. Beneficial or detrimental to both man's immaterial being and to his physiology.

***(Information adapted from MSBC 4343 Biblical Counseling Course at the College of Biblical Studies, Houston, Texas)***

## *Biblical Framework Counseling: Its Universals*

In his course of Biblical Counseling at the College of Biblical Studies Rich Thomson provides seven universal Truths by which the Biblical Framework operates. Here are more of His teachings on the Framework:

1. All people have an immaterial as well as a material aspect to their beings. It is in their immaterial beings (their souls and spirits – more commonly referred to in Scripture as their hearts) that they are qualitatively and uniquely different from the animals and in which they can relate to God (Genesis 1:26). In their immaterial beings, all people are responsible to God for the thoughts, attitudes, words, and actions for which the Word of God states they are responsible (Mark. 7:21-23).

Because the biblical counselor understands these truths, he differentiates in his mind between the things for which the counselee is responsible to God and the things for which he is not responsible (Job 1 & 2).

2. All people experience in their relationships and circumstances negative things which happen to them – for which they are not responsible to God (Job 1 & 2).

The biblical counselor's responses to the negative things which have happened to the counselee should be to "weep with those who weep" (Romans 12:15) and to "bear one another's burdens" (Galatians 6:2). Of course, positive things also happen to people, and in these the biblical counselor should "rejoice with those who rejoice" (Romans 12:15). Rarely, however, do people seek counsel because things are going well.

3. All people experience non-responsible reactions to the positive and negative things which happen to them. That is, they experience physiological pain (and pleasure), immaterial grief or sorrow (and joy), and the bodily feelings which accompany them. These reactions are not wrong, and human beings are not responsible to God for them (Ephesians 4:30, I Peter 2:23).

Here the biblical counselor's response should be the same as that above – empathy.

4. When positive or negative things affect them, all people entertain either unloving or loving attitudes in their hearts in response to them and in response to the pain (or pleasure) and/or grief (or joy) which they experience as a result. Human beings are responsible to God for these reactions (I Corinthians 13:4-7).

The biblical counselor's responsibility here is to praise the counselee's loving responses and – gently, at the appropriate time – to address the counselee's unloving responses as being sin before God (I Thessalonians 5:14).

5. All people have a conscience which accuses them of their wrong responses and choices in life and exonerates them of their right responses and choices (Romans 2:15). As a result of the work of their consciences, then, they normally experience these instinctive and instantaneous immaterial effects in their hearts: a consciousness of guilt and a sense of guilt, or a consciousness of not being guilty and a sense of peace; a consciousness of God's judgment and a fear of that judgment, or a consciousness of approval and a sense of confidence; a fleeing from that sense of judgment and from that sense of guilt, or a drawing near to God (Genesis 3:10-11, Proverbs 28:1, I John 4:18, Romans 2:14-15).

The biblical counselor's responsibility here is especially to recognize expressions of the negative effects in the counselee's life and to help him to understand and to deal with their root cause (Proverbs 20:5).

6. When people experience in their hearts a sense of guilt, a sense of judgment (usually experienced as apparently uncaused or disproportional fear – Prov. 28:1), or a fleeing from that sense of judgment (usually experienced as apparently uncaused or disproportional fleeing – Prov. 28:1), the only sufficient solution for the removal of these negative effects and their replacement with positive effects is a right relationship with the one true God made known through the Lord Jesus Christ (Hebrews 9:14, I John 3:21).

The biblical counselor's responsibility here is to help the counselee understand his need for the forgiveness and righteousness provided by the Lord Jesus Christ (if he is an unbeliever) or his need for confession of his sin (if he is a believer) and the filling of God's Spirit, which happens concurrently with them, and which produces God's *agapē* love in his heart (II Corinthians 5:21, I John 1:9, Ephesians 5:18, Galatians 5:22-23).

7. There are four basic ways in which all people relate to each other. At any given moment in any given relationship, they are either open and loving, open and unloving, closed and loving, or closed and unloving. (The unbeliever's love – reflected from God's good gifts in his life (James 1:17) – is but a faint representation of the love which the Holy Spirit produces in the believer's life.) (Proverbs 27:5-6.)

The biblical counselor's responsibility here is to help the counselee see the importance of openly expressing God's love back to God and to his fellow man – at the proper time and place – and to guide the counselee in practical ways of openly expressing that love.

***(Information adapted from MSBC 4343 Biblical Counseling Course at the College of Biblical Studies, Houston, Texas)***

# Counseling Comparison

In his course of Biblical Counseling at the College of Biblical Studies, Rich Thomson provides distinctions between Nouthetic Counseling and Biblical Framework Counseling:

> Both the Nouthetic Counselor and the Biblical Framework Counselor have the highest regard for the Word of God and are committed to the proposition that the Scripture has the answers for the non-organically induced problems of man. Both also compassionately bear the burdens of those who come for counsel, lovingly help them address any wrong attitudes or behaviors in their lives, and encourage them to be consistently filled with God's Spirit and grow in God's Word. There is, however, some difference in emphasis between them.
>
> In general, the Nouthetic Counselor individually assesses each problem presented to him, finds the heart and behavioral sin issues evident in it, and brings scriptural truth to bear on the problem – a sound, biblical approach.
>
> The Biblical Framework Counselor prefers to assess each problem presented to him with a more unified approach–one based upon a universal Biblical Framework unfolded in Scripture for understanding the inner workings of the human heart. Using this Biblical Framework, he is able to diagnose and to treat from the Word of God alone the root cause of both the common counseling problems and the great majority of the human mental disorders listed in the DSM-IV-TR.
>
> He is also able through the Framework to gain insight into features of mental disorder and deep personal problems that do not otherwise appear to be specifically addressed as sin in Scripture, and to recognize these features as resulting from unloving attitudes often not paid careful attention to, ignored, or justified in the heart.
>
> When giving God's answers to man's inner problems, the Biblical Framework Counselor stresses, among other things, the importance of walking in God's Spirit and in His *agapē* love for Him and for others, the four basic kinds of human relationship found in Scripture, and how to establish and maintain open loving relationships in all areas of life, to God's glory and to one's own blessing.

***(Information adapted from MSBC 4343 Biblical Counseling Course at the College of Biblical Studies, Houston, Texas)***

# BIBLIOGRAPHY

Adams, Jay. Biblical Counseling Manual, USA: Presbyterian & Reformed, 1973.

Adams, Jay. How to Help People Change, Grand Rapids: Zondervan 1986

MSBC 4343 Biblical Counseling Course at the College of Biblical Studies, Houston, Texas)

National Association of Nouthetic Counselors (Concept of the qualifications of a biblical counselor)

Thomson, Rich. The Heart of Man and The Mental Disorders, Houston: Biblical Counseling Ministries, Inc., 2004

Tripp, Paul David. Instruments in the Redeemer's Hands: People in Need of Change Helping People in Need of Change, Phillipsburg, NJ: P&R Publ., 2002.

Wayne Mack Ministries (Consent to Counsel Form)

www.ingramcontent.com/pod-product-compliance
Lightning Source LLC
Chambersburg PA
CBHW081257170426
43198CB00017B/2818